THE SUPER STUDS

by HOWARD ELSON

Hope this tickles you Dildo

Lots of love — To Pen

PROTEUS
London & New York

PROTEUS BOOKS is an imprint of
The Proteus Publishing Group

United States
PROTEUS PUBLISHING COMPANY, INC.
distributed to the trade by:
CHARLES SCRIBNER'S SONS
597 Fifth Avenue
New York, N.Y. 10017

United Kingdom
PROTEUS (PUBLISHING) LIMITED
Bremar House,
Sale Place,
London, W2 1PT

ISBN 0 906071 25 9

First published in US November 1980
First published in UK November 1980
© 1980 Howard Elson & Proteus Publishing Company.
All rights reserved.

Typeset by Computacomp (UK) Ltd.
Printed and bound in England.

Contents

1

Who's on next?

"I have had three or four girls in a single evening and I suppose in all I have made love to 3,000 women."

The words belong to French singing star Claude Francois who wrote the multi-million-selling song " 'My Way". And when it came to sex, Claude certainly *did* do it his way.

"Love is like drinking," he said. "When you are surrounded by beautiful wine, you tend to drink more and more."

He indulged himself as often as he possibly could, making love to an endless stream of young and willing wenches, all because he was convinced his actions would actually help him to *retain* his youth and vigor. Well, that was his story and he stuck to it.

When he died in March 1978 — he accidentally electrocuted himself after fitting a new light bulb into a faulty socket while standing in the bath — a macabre sex story circulated in the world's Press. It suggested that his body was far too weak to withstand even the mildest shock because only minutes before his demise, he had exhausted himself totally after a frantic sexual romp with *three nubile teenage girls*.

A superstud? Well ... the media certainly made him out to be one. They reported his sexual triumphs with much more gusto than they showed towards his other considerable talents. After all, it was his sex life the public longed to read about ...

John Fitzgerald Kennedy, the thirty-fifth President of the United States of America, was a reputed philanderer and womanizer. Not content to be married to one of the world's most beautiful and most desirable women, so the stories go, Kennedy was almost obsessed with sex. He is said to have enjoyed extra-marital affairs with a string of willing partners. During his tragically short term of office, rumors abounded that

JFK was frequently jumping in and out of White House beds with anyone who was available *and* discreet — including many famous actresses — to satisfy his incredible sexual appetite! Kennedy treated sex in a very matter-of-fact way, but could never remain faithful. To him variety was always the spice of life and he tasted it as often as he possibly could.

A superstud? Well ... The Press was sitting on a whole mountain of true stories about Kennedy's sexual furore, with names, dates and places readily available. It didn't print them. Yet after he was assassinated, the stories came out and rumors started to fly in the Press and in books, all adding to his legendary sexual prowess.

In the golden silent days of Hollywood, director William Desmond Taylor was reputed to be "Sin City's" leading Lothario. He was rumored to have squired many of Hollywood's most glamorous leading ladies, and some of the legendary movie queens of the day. Taylor kept lasting souvenirs of each sexual conquest. Locked in a cupboard in his bedroom were the trophies of his particular kind of big game hunting — various forms of women's underwear, each one displaying the initials of its owner with the date the sexual encounter took place, tagged to them. The cupboard was packed to capacity.

A superstud? Well ... when he was mysteriously murdered, the media went to town exposing the so-called chaste young actresses who had succumbed to Taylor's charms. They also had a field day when they discovered he had been carrying on affairs with *four* women simultaneously and that several years previously, he had deserted his wife and daughter.

Yet, surely if anyone deserved the right to the title "superstud", it must certainly have been the unlikely sounding Moulay Ismail — the last Sharifian Emperor of Morocco — and he could prove it!

According to legend and that most respected organ of fascinating information, The Guinness Book Of Records, Ismail sired no less than *eight hundred and eighty eight children* (548 boys, 340 girls) in his fifty seven years. He was born in 1672 and during his lifetime was renowned throughout North Africa and beyond as "Ismail — The Blood Thirsty", though what he did to gain such a reputation isn't well known. However, it is incredible he ever found the time — or the energy — to gain such notoriety!

Throughout history, it does seem that the more women a man can make love to, the more highly regarded he appears in the eyes of a prying world. Women desire the sexual athletes; men just look on in admiration; and the media eagerly laps it all up. And in the main, many of the most illustrious and famous men of the past have been remembered, not only for the contributions they made to the history of the world, but also for their achievements between the blankets. In many cases, it was their sexual escapades that made them famous in the first place. Or infamous!

Casanova de Seingalt Giovanni Giacomo has been remembered for just one thing — a totally dissolute existence. He not only gave his life to a sexual mania and the pursuit of female flesh in all its naked glory, he also gave his *name*.

Still, once a person has crossed the threshold from obscurity to fame — in no matter what field he establishes himself — his life becomes almost public property and rife for the intrusive eye of the media. If there are any skeletons in the cupboards, so much the better, particularly sexual ones. It often seems that the media is obsessed with sex!

For a good many years now, words like "playboy", "womanizer", "lady killer",

"Casanova" and, more recently, "superstud", have been banded about certainly by the Press as if they belong to an endangered species with extinction looming over the horizon. And it appears that any man in the public eye – who has displayed the merest hint of macho-ness – has only to be seen in the company of a woman, to have the superstud tag thrust upon him. It's a game the media adores playing ... and they do it quite well.

And the media can, and often does, make and break reputations – though it is the latter mainly that sells newspapers and books. A fickle public clamors for information on their favorite showbusiness stars, and adores stories where the slightest hint of scandal and sex is involved. The public *wants* to know which famous star is doing what to whom ... and where and when and how often! The media is only too happy to supply the information and latest titbits of news. It has kept the diary editors and gossip-columnists in business for many, many years now. Almost overnight, through the right – or the wrong – publicity in the Press, a reputation can be established.

Omar Sharif, himself a prime target for the media and a candidate in the stud-stakes, puts it into perspective: "I have a very normal sex-life, even sub-standard. Most men do as well, if not better. The only difference is that they don't read about it in the newspapers the next day."

Burt Reynolds echoes humorously: "I sometimes have to look at the newspapers to find out who I am currently supposed to be dating."

Oliver Tobias, who starred in the title role in the movie "The Stud", tries hard to live down the reputation the Press saddled him with after the film was released. He says: "Just after the film, girls were always coming up to me, making it quite clear what they wanted. I still get girls throwing themselves at me. That's the trouble, the romance has gone. There's no more real feeling. It's just knickers off and go."

And that certainly does prove that once an image is created by the media, the name sticks ... it's there for life, or until the next one comes along. After all, wasn't it the media, albeit a Russian news agency, that coined the phrase (and ultimately created the image), "The Iron Lady" when describing British Prime Minister Margaret Thatcher? It was a theme taken up immediately by all the world's newspapers.

However, it does work the other way, and the media can – and often is – manipulated. Indeed, several of today's pop and movie heart-throbs are in fact homosexual – some, despite being married *and* giving the outward appearance of being the epitome of the masculine dream. If the truth were known, and names were named, many thousands of women's dreams and illusions would be shattered.

In the glory days of Hollywood, during the 1930's and 1940's, the great studio publicity machine was all-powerful and all-important to a film industry, whose aim was to keep the movie-land tinsel well polished and always shining. The PR boys regularly created brand new identities for their stars, making "super" people out of very ordinary, mundane actors and actresses ... who just happened to land a lucky break. (Or slept with the producer, but that's another story). The truth was regularly pre-fabricated and packaged in sparkle – a veritable gospel according to MGM or Twentieth Century Fox – to keep the all American dream alive.

Clark Gable's "official" Hollywood biography referred to his background as being Irish-Dutch. In truth, he came from pure German-stock, which would certainly have been bad for business, and his career, during the 1930's when Hitler was stirring up a

European hornet's nest. Anti-German feeling in America had reached fever pitch at that time and the "King" definitely wouldn't have become the "Kaiser" ... he would just have faded into the obscurity from which he came.

The publicity boys were also called in to protect the studios' properties by *covering up* many of their star's outrageous misdemeanors, which if a hint of scandal had ever leaked to the media, would have made front pages and closed the curtains on their careers. Hollywood stars, generally speaking, were wholesome people – apart from Errol Flynn who was a law unto himself and a bottle of vodka – and the publicity people kept them that way for as long as they were valuable to the studios.

It's almost the same today, for with Machiavellian publicity campaigns reaching new heights, nothing displayed in the Press, or heard on the radio, or seen on the screen, is quite as simple as it appears. However, today's stars often have love-hate relationships with the intrusive media. Sure, they are only too happy to oblige the Press when they need the publicity to help their careers – they are only too eager to talk about themselves when they are on the first rung of the ladder trying to establish themselves. Yet, once they *have* "made it" and become established, the happy smiling face disappears in a wave of accusations that the media is too prying! Though "stars" in this context is a word with ever-widening meaning.

Nowadays, statesmen, politicians, doctors, writers and businessmen from all walks of life, are angling for column inches in the same way as the more traditional entertainers and sportsmen. Everything today is given the showbusiness treatment: the hard sell, the glitter and the sparkle, and the razz matazz. Everyone today is very conscious of the *right* image, and PR men abound. And the most popular image of them all – for men that is – is the virile male, macho man, and *homosuperstudus*. It sells – and the media loves it and helps to create it.

Men like Canadian premier Pierre Trudeau, entrepreneur Gunther Sachs, magazine magnate Victor Lownes, and Phillipe Junot – the businessman husband of Princess Caroline of Monaco – have all been dubbed as "playboys" by the media eager for stories on this new "jet" set. They have waxed lyrical over their sex-ploits to such an extent that they have all become personalities in their own right in the eyes of the public, alongside the stars of stage, screen and sports field. There have been many others. ...

As soon as Henry Kissinger was discovered by Richard Nixon in the late 1960's as his very own Svengali for world peace, the media latched on to him immediately. He was refreshingly different. He had flair, panache and style. When they discovered that he also had a penchant for beautiful women (he did nothing to conceal his sexual preferences and even worked overtime to cultivate the publicity), almost at once, he emerged as "The Playboy Of The Western Wing" as Time magazine called him. Britain's *Daily Express* described him as "This Man Of Affairs" and the *Guardian* thought he had "masculine glamor, film star quality. In short the Henry Kissinger of today dazzles."

Before his second marriage, to Nancy Maginnis, in 1974, Henry Kissinger's sexual diary was an open secret which made world headlines. Every new sexual conquest – there were many for Henry liked to shop around for variety and his little black book was famous and bulged with names and numbers from all over the world – was eagerly unveiled to the public via the media. One paper said he had "the most publicized love life in the world." Henry didn't comment, he was too busy. As one of his girl friends put it: "Henry's never too busy for sex, though."

Actress Jill St. John was a constant companion, and many people believed they would eventually marry. He even introduced her to the Russian leader Leonid Breznev. It was also revealed in a Sunday newspaper, that Kissinger always phoned her immediately after emerging from top secret, top-level discussions with the world leaders in Moscow, Paris, Rome or Damascus.

"I think he just wanted to talk to me to relax a little after those exhausting discussions," she said, and then added:

"He tells me: 'don't worry, Jill. Even if I lost the book, I'll still call you because I carry *your* number around in my head.' "

Their affair made the headlines all over the world and they were often seen together walking hand in hand. She called him "cuddly" and he liked her because she had an IQ of 164 and could understand the complexities of his mission. Yet, their liaison did have a few difficulties.

"You can't risk pecking him on the cheek in the back of a limousine because you know darned well there's a cadillac behind filled with security people straining their necks to see what's going on," she complained.

Miss St. John, however, was just one of what seemed like an endless line of actresses all vying for Henry's attentions. It suited him.

"I go out with actresses because I'm not very apt to marry one," he said. "I also like Hollywood starlets, they are even greater egomaniacs than I am. They talk about themselves the whole time and I don't have to talk about myself."

But Henry also fraternized with a much more selective and much more star-studded cast, including Scandinavian actress Liv Ullman, who called him "gracious and friendly. A gallant man."

Then there was Candice Bergan who found him "fascinating"; Claire Bloom; Gina Lollobrigida; and James Bond beauties Ursula Andress and Maud Adams. *And* Marlo Thomas, Ruta Lee and Angel Tompkins.

Samantha Eggar said: "I think he likes me because I make him laugh. But he's always complaining about the way I treat him. He's truly an extraordinary man."

Zsa Zsa Gabor told a newspaper: "Dahling, he is the most marvellous man. I love him. But all the time the White House send him radio signals. Can you imagine having a husband who goes bleep all the time?"

Kissinger's attitude was crisply philosophical: "When these ladies start using me for publicity, that is when I decide to terminate a relationship." It was an easy get out if he ever wanted to take it. Henry Kissinger, and all who sailed with him, was submerged by the great publicity machine. Everything he did was scrutinized, and no matter what he said, there was no getting away from it.

Henry's tastes in women were very "Catholic" to say the least, and they didn't end with actresses. He was involved with Playboy nudie-model June Wilkinson. There was Hollywood agent Sue Mengers and TV journalist Barbara Howar, another candidate tipped to become the second Mrs. Kissinger. Producer Margaret Osmar said: "His greatest charm is his sense of humor."

Journalist Joyce Haler echoed: "He's worldly, humorous, sophisticated, always a cavalier with women."

But that wasn't a view shared by French TV producer Danielle Hunebelle, who was so distressed when he finished their affair, that she wrote a book about him called "Dear Henry", cataloging his "little habits".

Henry Kissinger — who was born in the German town of Fürth in 1923 and fled to America in 1938 from the Nazi regime — possessed a fantastic magnetism over members of the opposite sex, but just *what* that attraction was and how it worked, baffled many people, including Martha Mitchell.

"I like Henry," she said. "And John (her husband) thought he was intelligent, but we've never been able to fathom out what other women apparently see in him."

It was a point taken up by a leading newspaper "Not even the doctor's most fervent admirers would argue that his appearance is heart-stopping." Though perhaps it was the awe-inspiring power he wielded that had them in raptures. Henry thought so: "There seems to be a certain aphrodisiac quality about power.

Kissinger was always very open about his relationships with women, and often talked to the media about them.

"After work I try to be with a beautiful girl, if possible not too intelligent. After an afternoon with Indira Gandhi, I certainly don't want to spend the evening with Golda Meir," he told one newspaper reporter.

To another he said: "If a girl's bored with me, she thinks its her own fault!"

... And he found his playboy image both amusing and helpful.

"I think it's useful in diplomacy because it reminds people I'm not some fuddy museum piece," he laughed.

"My frivolous reputation is overdone of course, as we all know. To me women are a pleasing pastime, a hobby. I'd be a fool to devote all my energies to a hobby wouldn't I? I am too much in love with my work. I find that completely satisfying."

Since then, of course, Henry Kissinger has married once again and taken something of a back seat in the political arena following the fall from power of, first Richard Nixon, and then Gerald Ford. But he still keeps at least one eye on the opposite sex, while the media keeps a watchful eye on him.

In 1976, while his wife Nancy was away on a two-week tour of Australia, Henry was seen in the company of Elizabeth Taylor at a star-studded charity gala in Washington. It was an innocuous incident, but the media gave it the full treatment. Within a few hours of the event, the "liaison" had received world-wide coverage.

For Henry Kissinger — once hailed in the Press as the "Superkraut Playboy" — old habits died hard. ...

Like Kissinger, Hugh Hefner's origins were German, though his mother came from Sweden. He was a humble advertising copy-writer from a strict puritanical Methodist background, before he devised what was to become the multi-billion selling magazine *Playboy*, in 1953. It changed not only his life dramatically, but the lives of millions of men (and women) all over the world.

Playboy was the magazine the world had been waiting for. It proved a blazing beacon for the sexually liberated ... and led the permissive revolution.

Hefner was sitting on a goldmine of bums and boobs, with a license virtually to print money. He became a multi-millionaire himself, and set about establishing a vast sexual empire across the globe, including the famous Playboy Clubs — the first of which was opened in 1960 when Hefner gave the world the Bunny Girl — which he headed like an Emperor of the Erotic!

And like his predecessors from the heady days of the Roman Empire, Hugh Hefner revelled in his own real-life sexual fantasies to become the epitome of the all-American macho male ... and one of the most envied men in the world. He was a natural target for the media and he encouraged the publicity with the same verve with which he supposedly made love — if the many kiss-and-tell revelations from pin-up girls that have frequently appeared in the newspapers, are to be believed.

His life-style, quite simply, was fantastic, and not surprisingly attracted Press like flies round a honey pot. He flew the world in a luxury DC9 aircraft — the "Big Bunny" — which was re-furbished to his own designs and specifications, and equipped with *everything* he could possibly need to satisfy any desire, including his own particular brand of air hostesses.

His luxury 50-roomed mansion in Chicago was unique, containing fabulously designed and sumptuously furnished rooms, *and* featuring a full-sized swimming pool, encased in glass so that Hef could watch nude girls swimming underwater. There were sophisticated whirlpool baths, steam rooms and saunas ... and a sunken Roman-styled bath which could accommodate an army of people, particularly young girls. And *much, much* more. It was a case of decadence gone wild.

Hefner's own bedroom was a masterpiece. It featured a vast playing field of a bed which was covered entirely in mink. It was so designed that it could move through three hundred and sixty degrees, and adopt almost any position. Trained on to the bed was Hefner's own video film system, allowing him to be filmed, while making love to his bevy of beauties ... for his very own sexy home movies, or maybe a training manual! Mirrors covered the walls and ceilings, and erotic pictures and art were prominently displayed ... all to give mood and atmosphere to the room! It was a veritable sexpalace, fit for a veritable king of sex.

And, of course, some of his Playboy Playmates of the Month, and Year, were also available to render Hef their own particular kind of service! He was, after all, reputed to have made love to the majority of them, including such girls as Janet Pilgrim, Karen Christy, Marilyn Cole — who became the first *full frontal nude* ever to appear in *Playboy*'s centerfold and later added to Hefner's vast reputation and sexual image by selling her sex memoirs to Britain's *Daily Mirror* — Connie Kresky, Barbie Benton, and Miss January, Miss February, Miss March, Miss April ... All of whom *he* had discovered — in more ways than one — and put all their charms on display in glorious full color before the eyes of an eager world.

The more publicity he and his lifestyle received, the better. It sold magazines ... and the media played a vital part in helping create a living, loving legend. Hefner, of course, was delighted.

Christiaan Barnard was a moderately distinguished heart specialist within his own particular circle in South Africa until 1967 when he, too, hit the publicity jackpot after performing the world's first heart transplant operation. Then in almost one fell swoop, he became, as one newspaper commented: "The Superstar Surgeon". Another added: "The world of beautiful women was open to Barnard from the moment he surfaced socially from the operating theater." He emerged as a real live Doctor Kildare whose nurses called him "heart-throb Chris" behind his back, and has been described as "the doctor with the greatest-ever bedside manner." It was easy to see why, too.

Barnard was young, good-looking and trendy. He certainly brought the image of the medical profession out of the shadows and into the 20th Century.

One chronicler of the exploits of "beautiful people" commented: "If you didn't know he was Doctor Barnard, you might well mistake him for an international playboy ... or South Africa's answer to Gregory Peck.

"He is, on his own defiant admission, a lively swinger. Given the choice of spending his leisure in the company of the young and beautiful, or the old and professional, he goes where the frollicking action is."

And if that "frollicking action" contained beautiful young girls, then so much the better. It certainly kept Chris happy *and* supplied the world's newspapers with a string of good stories and front page pictures. With the rapidity of a gatling gun, his name was linked romantically with dozens of dazzling movie starlets and glamorous ladies from all over the world.

There was German actress Uta Levka; his own PR girl Cathy Bildton; millionaire's daughter Johanna Rayan; and Barbara Zoeller, who later became his wife and the second Mrs. Barnard.

In France, he was photographed in a compromising position in the back of a taxi with a beautifully good looking girl — and when he saw the cameramen, he ducked down out of sight! He also spent many hours in the company of Doris Kleiner, the former wife of Yul Brynner.

In Italy, Sophia Loren entertained him and actually devised a dish in his honor — the ultimate compliment — calling it Lasagne Pasticatta a la Christiaan Barnard. *And* the celebrated actress Rosanno Schiaffino was another beauty who vied for his attentions.

Chris said at the time of his womanizing wonderlust: "I'm naturally and normally happy with women. And why shouldn't I be? I get hundreds of letters from all kinds of women."

His first wife Louwtjie, however, told a Sunday newspaper: "Like King Henry (VIII), Christiaan Barnard had a weakness for women — admittedly always for exceptionally attractive women.

"These women did not mean more to him than prey means to a big game hunter. As soon as one fell for him, he was no longer interested, he turned around and went after the next prey."

Barnard's most famous, and much publicized affair, was with the Italian movie star Gina Lollobrigida, who called him "lollipop" and admitted that he asked her to marry him.

"He heaped orchids and roses on me and I fell in love, too," she said.

Their liaison hit the headlines throughout the world when a newspaper published a series of love letters supposedly written by La Lollo to her doctor lover. They caused a sensation, not un-naturally, in Italy and South Africa, though Gina filed a lawsuit against the publication to try and stem the rumors. Still, it didn't stop their intimate secrets being splashed across the front pages. In one letter she said: "Our love is too deep for doing craziness!" Another she wrote of being "wild with love" for Chris, "unable to eat and sleep" and she couldn't live without him.

The affair, which certainly contributed to the break up of Barnard's first marriage, finally ended when Gina accused him of "telling the world" about their relationship. "I soon realized he was just seeking publicity,'' she said at the time.

Christiaan Barnard's extraordinary talent for courting publicity often worked against him. In 1970, the University of Salonica in Greece, cancelled a decision to award him an honorary degree, saying that in their eyes, he wasn't a ''serious man, just a playboy''.

It definitely *didn't* help his cause for respectability, when rumors circulated shortly afterwards in the media, that the Hollywood film moguls were interested in filming his colorful life story, with Gregory Peck playing the lead. A few months later, it was announced that *he* was set to star in a film of his own ... and a *musical* at that! It wasn't any wonder that he was openly accused, time and time again, of purposely seeking publicity for his own ends. It was something, however, he denied vehemently.

''I would dare any other man to have been in my position and avoided the publicity,'' he said. ''This is something I didn't look for. If I really looked for it, I would have had cameras in the operating theater.

''I do *resent* the interest shown in my private life. I don't care how much of a celebrity you are, a certain amount of your private life should be your own.''

He raged his own love-hate relationship against the media.

Yet, he confided in a British Sunday newspaper: ''Doctors are human. The only difficulty is that the world is watching one enjoy what other medical men enjoy in privacy. That's the price I have to pay. My personal life has gone under the microscope as much as my medical activities, and I do resent it terribly. If I'm seen drinking, I'm a playboy. If I'm seen with a girl, well ... it's for the worst.

''The only thing I sometimes yearn for, is what I had once. And that's *obscurity*. I never realized how great it was to be a nobody surgeon.''

A reluctant superstud – as he once said, only ''sometimes''.

This book is a celebration for ten of the men who over the last sixty-odd years – rightly or wrongly – have become known in the eyes of the world, and hailed by the media, as *womanizers* ... *lady killers* ... *Casanovas* ... *superstuds!* The men, and the myths. The facts, and the fantasy. The lovers, and the legends, whose common denominator is an amazing attraction to women, and an incredible power over them.

However, it goes a lot deeper. For they are linked in many other ways, too. Indeed, several of them have made love (passionately or otherwise) to many of the same women though *not* at the same time. At the last count, Britt Ekland and Anouk Aimee led the field. *And* most of them had very serious affairs – in some cases resulting in marriage – with *older* women!

All ten macho heroes have at one time or another exceled on the sports field! Errol Flynn was a brilliant tennis player, while Clark Gable's sport was baseball. Warren Beatty and Burt Reynolds were both offered contracts to become professional grid-iron football stars, while Omar Sharif and Rod Stewart preferred the more subtle game of soccer. Boxing captivated Jean Paul Belmondo and Ryan O'Neal, though in the latter's case it still proves a great attraction. Tom Jones has proved himself an all-round athlete, and the legendary ''Great Lover'' of the silent screen, Rudolph Valentino, had a great talent for gymnastics ... and dancing the tango!

That's not all ...

Several of these superstuds came from distinguished family backgrounds, and many had, if not celebrated fathers, certainly figures who commanded great respect in their community. Jean Paul Belmondo's father was a very distinguished and famous sculptor. Errol Flynn's was a highly-decorated scientist and biologist. Burt Reynolds' was the local chief of Police, and Warren Beatty's was a High School Principal. Omar Sharif's father was a rich and influential timber merchant, while Valentino's was a vetinary surgeon. And Ryan O'Neal's was a famous scriptwriter.

A psychologist would have a field day.

They say that all the world loves a lover and it is particularly true about the superstuds. They have won their spurs of admiration not only from members of their own sex, who admire them and would like the opportunity of emulating them, but from women, as well, who wonder at their reputations … and desire them. They would love the chance to find out if the rumors *are* true!

However, it doesn't quite work out the other way around.

Even in this liberated age of permissiveness and sexual equality, if a woman got up to the same kind of sexual athletics as her male counterparts, and made love at the drop of a hat to a string of eligible men, she would be frowned upon by the world. Far from gaining a saucy reputation — admiration from the male populus; envy from the female — she would definitely be labelled as a *hussy* or a *nymphomaniac*, a *slut* or a *slag*, or a *whore* … words that don't exactly reek of charm.

So, it just goes to consolidate the old adage that it really *is* different for a man.

Still, there are many lady superstuds — they really must devise a suitable way to describe themselves. Somehow words like *superstudette*, *superlay*, *temptress* don't exactly conjure up the same kind of meaning. And they have all lived equally colorful and incident-packed lives as their male counterparts. They can definitely tell a tale or two of their own sex-capades between the blankets. The media has certainly kept us all very well informed over the years.

But that, as they say, is another story, for another time.

2
ERROL FLYNN
...The Robin Hood of the bedroom

Errol Flynn was without doubt, one of the most rampant superstuds in the history of the bedroom.

He had all the qualifications, too. He was devastatingly good-looking — until his handsomeness was devoured by drugs and the drink. He had a magnificent physique, amazing staying power between the sheets and a personality that oozed charm and sex appeal.

Women adored him, even though as David Niven said — "he treated them like playthings to be discarded without warning for new models." They often queued for his sexual handouts, and Flynn actually thought *nothing* of bedding two and even *three* girls in one session. He regularly boasted of making love to over 10,000 women, though not all at the same time. Even *his* bed wasn't big enough."

Errol was good, too, and he knew it. He revelled in the image that had been created all around him. "The public has always expected me to be a playboy and a decent chap never lets his public down", he said, and he was always true to his word and rarely disappointed his public. They had a picture of a gentlemanly rogue, which had been painted by Flynn, and landscaped by the world's newspapers. A lady-killer who bedded almost every woman he ever came in contact with. And Errol obliged, why shouldn't he? He was on to a good thing, and in his case all publicity was good publicity.

It appeared in the papers at least, that he moved in and out of bedrooms with the same ease and grace that he displayed as Robin Hood swinging from tree to tree in Hollywood's Sherwood Forest when he starred in his most famous of all films (and possibly one of the all-time great movies) — "The Adventures of Robin Hood".

Besides his women, though, Errol had another great passion in his life — the sea. He

took great delight in exploring his beloved oceans, which he regularly referred to as his "mistresses" and the only ones who would ever tame him. When he purchased the 120-foot luxury yacht "Zaca", the ship's house flag became a crowing rooster, a rampant cock! "A symbol of what I have become to the world," he said. He never said a truer word!

When it came to women, Errol had a penchant for young girls — the younger the better, between the ages of thirteen and sixteen preferably. He couldn't get enough of them. It was unfortunately this obsession with ridiculously young girls — he often spent his time outside girls' schools just ogling the pupils — that was to cause one of the great Hollywood scandals in the 1940's, when Errol was charged with statutory rape.

Some people have also hinted that he liked young *boys*, and that he had various passionate homosexual relationships during his lifetime, which might well be true. Errol was a great one for experimenting with the pleasures (any pleasures) of life. It would be an honest bet to say that he tried almost everything once, and if he liked the experience, he continued with it. If not ... who knows. Perhaps he did experiment with homosexual relationships. Perhaps he *was* looking for something out of the ordinary to satisfy his needs. Perhaps he needed another kind of stimulant. But if he *did* have affairs with people of his own sex — particularly young boys as has been suggested — then he was very discreet about it all, and had to be! For a man with his reputation as a lady-killer and superstud would have been crucified in the newspapers, and his career would certainly have come to an abrupt end. Yet there was hardly a whisper.

Flynn simply lived life to the full, exactly the way *he* wanted to live it! If anything, or anyone got in his way, hard luck. He was having a ball and he didn't mind who knew it, or who got hurt along the way!

Yet despite having everything going for him, he still managed to blow it. He made a fortune from his movies, but the various women in his life took great pleasure in relieving him of it — and he ended up broke, down and out and on skid row, suffering from an excess of hard living. It was a tragedy but he'd brought it on himself. The booze, the drugs and the women had certainly helped to take their toll.

In the end, however, deserted by most of his friends, he still managed to get his priorities right and found a beautiful, young, seventeen year old girl with whom to spend his dying days! The cockerel might well have been dying ... but it was still rampant!

He was born Errol Leslie Thomson Flynn in Hobart, Tasmania, on June 20th, 1909.

He adored his father — Theodore Flynn who was Professor of zoology and marine biology at Hobart University. However, there was little love lost between Errol and Morelle, his mother. They didn't get on together at all.

Even as a youngster Flynn was an adventurer, and regularly experimented with every new thing he discovered. When he went a little too far in his experiments with the little girl next door and was discovered by her mother, who in turn told Morelle of her son's "disgusting behavior", Errol ran away from home after a bitter row. He was seven years old and spent several days on the run, fending for himself. It was a talent he became very good at later in his life.

At thirteen, he discovered, to his delight, the wonders of sex for the first time, when he went all the way with the baby-sitter — who was slightly older than the boy, and just a touch more experienced in these matters.

And at sixteen, after his "formal" education had been taken in Tasmania, England and mainland Australia, he was expelled from school, when the headmaster finally ran out of patience with him and could stand his hell-raising — which included playing truant, seducing various local maidens, and fighting with various local schoolfriends — no longer, even if his father *was* by this time a celebrated man of science, and making a name for himself in England.

A year later, Flynn was off on the adventure trail once more, to seek his fortune in the gold fields of New Guinea. It was 1926.

New Guinea was just the place for a foot-loose and fancy-free adventurer, with rugged good looks and a body to match, and a talent for lying and cheating whenever it was called for. He joined Government service as a cadet and was put in charge of monitoring the sanitary requirements of part of the island. The job however, didn't last very long, for when he was caught literally with his pants down in a very uncompromising position, making love to the wife of a top Government official ... he was dismissed! *And* lost his pension. Still, the country was lithe and exciting, just like a woman's body — and Flynn knew all about that. He also wanted to explore every single contour. Besides, he was young and for a man of his talents — whatever they were at that time — even *he* didn't really know, apart from an ability to make love for as long as he wanted to — something just *had* to come up.

It did — time and time again.

Flynn spent half a dozen years on and off the island, during which time he spread his talents working on copra and tobacco plantations. He also bought and sold shares in various gold fields in the mountains and traded in illegal native laborers to work them — for which he was jailed on at least one occasion. Much later, he bought half-ownership in a boat called "Sirocco" on which he sailed up and down the coast-line, hiring it out to anyone who could afford the fees. *And*, later still, he made his acting debut, playing the part of Fletcher Christian, in a film called "In The Wake Of The Bounty", which was made in Tahiti. It was a case of extreme irony. In real life, he was actually descended from Christian through his mother's line of ancestry.

But of all the many things the island bestowed upon the rapidly maturing male, one had a most profound effect on him, which lasted throughout his life. The exciting and under-developed country gave him a passion for young, nubile girls. Native girls of all shapes and sizes were readily available (even for trade or barter) and Errol certainly had his share, so much so, that he inherited something else from his over indulgence — the black pox, a serious form of venereal disease. That, too, was something that was to crop up on several occasions in later life. Still, it was a risk — and Errol loved gambling!

Although New Guinea was his base of operations — which all the time included making money as simply and as quickly as possible because he was always broke — Flynn made many trips back to the mainland of Australia and on one such occasion, he met a very rich, very elegant society lady several years his senior. She was married, but no matter — and showed a remarkable interest in the young adventurer. He was convinced she would seduce him, and of course, she didn't let him down.

They spent many nights of passion together — "she taught me so much", he admitted. "She was my first experience of what a *real* woman could mean."

However, even that didn't stop him robbing her of a small fortune in diamond and platinum jewelry one night while the lady slept, no doubt dreaming of waves thundering on the shore, following a typical night of steamy love-making.

Now with the wherewithal to get his hands on a substantial amount of money for the first time in his life, he headed back to New Guinea, where he knew that not only could he sell the jewels, but he could buy even more shares in the gold plantations, more cheap native labor to work them, and even more young girls to warm his bed. Hopefully, he would strike it lucky!

He got as far as Brisbane – broke again, apart from the goodies hidden about his person which he daren't sell for fear of discovery. So he took a temporary job mining in the desert to replenish funds for the trip back to the island. Two months later he landed a job on a nearby sheep farm, where he had the distasteful occupation of de-sexing six-month old male lambs with his teeth! The job didn't last long either, much to his undoubted relief, and again it was his wandering eye and his incapacity to say "no" to a member of the opposite sex, that let him down. When he was discovered in bed with the farm owner's daughter, he was forced to make a hasty exit – stage left – with his pants in his hands and a shotgun at his rear.

He made it, but only just, out of Australia and back to the gold mines of New Guinea where he felt safe, at least from the outstretched arm of one outraged father. But it wasn't long before, using the proceeds of the sale of the jewelry, he was up to his old tricks again, recruiting illegal natives for labor and selling then at inflated prices to the prospectors. This time, however, his little racket had been discovered and Government agents were hot on his trail ... and closing in for an arrest! Flynn made the only sensible decision open to him and left the country, fast! He set off in search of adventure yet again. It was 1932.

A year later he arrived in England, broke as usual. On the way, though, his lust for adventure had taken him in and out of bedrooms in Hong Kong – where one of his conquests tricked him out of all his money after introducing him to the wonders of opium – India, Africa and France. You can say one thing for Flynn, he did a great job in advancing the course of international relations.

It was in London that he decided to turn his hand to acting in order to make a career. That brief appearance as Fletcher Christian had inspired him, and now he desperately wanted to prove to himself that he had the makings of a good actor. At first it was a hard slog, but he was convinced he had the makings of a star. No-one else shared his optimism. So he had to lower his sights, and joined a repertory company in Northampton where he spent eighteen months playing a wide variety of parts, besides bedding a wide variety of his leading ladies. Northampton was never quite the same after he left.

After provincial repertory, Errol returned to London and made two undistinguished appearances on the West End stage where he was at last "discovered". Irving Asker – head of Warner Brothers Pictures in England – was impressed with his acting ability, and offered him a part in the movie "Murder at Monte Carlo". The finished product was seen by Jack Warner, himself, who in turn summoned Flynn to Hollywood. Errol had come up smelling of rose water once more. ...

Jack Warner later told an American newspaper how he came across the young actor. "I saw Errol Flynn one day in our London studios doing a bit part. I didn't know if the guy could act but he was handsomer than hell and radiated charm. So I hired him on impulse for $150 a week. Back in Hollywood he hung around for months doing nothing. We tested him for "Captain Blood", I signed Robert Donat to the part, but we had a $20,000 misunderstanding about payment, and he turned it down. Good thing, too, because as soon as I saw Flynn's test, I knew he had it. We gave him $300 a week for the part — it made him a star."

Errol Flynn set off for America convinced he was going to become a big star. On board the liner Paris, he met two women who were both to play their parts later on in his life. Lily Damita was a fiery French actress, eight years his senior, whom he later married. She was rumored to be bi-sexual and even actor David Niven noted that she spent much of her time surrounded by homosexuals!

The other lady in question was a Russian Princess — Flynn never discriminated against nationality and class — whom he seduced in New York and got more than he bargained for! After a night of conventional love-making, the Princess introduced our intrepid hero to the wonders of *sadism* by attacking him with a metal hairbrush! Errol didn't much care for the experience and made a hasty retreat from her bed, covered in blood! He didn't repeat the exercise.

He arrived in Hollywood almost completely unknown, but that was nothing new for Flynn and he didn't mind at all. It didn't take him too long to establish himself either. He had done it all many times before in many different places. But with every new movie he made, his name and reputation increased. He became one of Hollywood's top box-office attractions in a very short space of time. Women adored him on the screen as the daringly romantic rascal with a romantic twinkle in his eye. Millions of men admired him, too, as a symbol of what they always wanted to become themselves, but were never able to. They envied his off-screen activities, squiring the world's most beautiful women.

Flynn … loved it all. The women. The revelry. The reputation. He once said — "I allow myself to be understood as a colorful fragment in a drab world." And he worked hard at projecting his image.

He was a great practical joker. He once put a dead snake into the costume knickers of Olivia de Havilland during the filming of "The Charge Of The Light Brigade". She knew nothing of the intruder in her drawers even when she put them on and went out on to the set. Then, she suddenly discovered the creature and, thinking it was still alive and about to attack her, she jumped into a nearby pond and tried to drown it. Her relationship with Errol was never quite the same after that! But Flynn adored her — and often longed to seduce her, away from the big screen. Many of his friends believed that Olivia was his only true love — and she virtually rejected him.

On another occasion, he invited a high-ranking, yet boorish, Washington politician to a Hollywood party he was throwing. When the diplomat arrived at the front door, he was greeted by the maid, wearing little else than a pair of shoes, a pair of stockings and a big wide smile. She showed him into the "undressing room", where she told him to take off all his clothes — it was *that* kind of party. Then she would show him where the action was taking place. Naturally, the diplomat was delighted to be involved in such revelry that promised high jinks and so much more. He hurriedly discarded his clothes and stood, naked, waiting for the maid's return. The next moment, she opened the door to the dining room where the party was taking place, and announced his name. The politician, eager to get involved, marched merrily into

the room, only to be greeted by two dozen or more people dressed in full evening dress!

When he started to establish himself as a force-to-be-reckoned-with in Hollywood, Errol Flynn was living with Lily Damita, whom he called 'Tiger Lil'. Even in Los Angeles at that time, famous for its open morals and hard living, Flynn and his mistress, and their open-secret affair, were regularly the targets of the Press and gossip columns. But when they finally married, it was probably the worst thing that could have happened to him, in the long run particularly. And right from the beginning the marriage was set on a reckless course to disaster.

Errol, however, was never one to be tied down to one woman alone. "Women won't let me stay single, and I won't let myself stay married," he said, and then set about chasing every available girl in sight. He moved out of the marital home in the Hollywood Hills, and set up a bachelor apartment at 601 North Linden Drive, Beverley Hills – a house he rented from actress Rossalind Russell – with his old friend David Niven. They became the two most sexually potent men in the movie capital of the world ... never still, and never wanting to be.

Niven described the apartment as a hot bed of fun and bad behavior, and added, "the booze flowed freely, the girls formed an ever-changing pattern." And drugs and dope often flowed freely, too, for by then, Errol was heavily involved with narcotics, experimenting with anything he could get his hands on. It was strictly a singularly occupational hazard, Niven never indulged.

"In those pre-war days, Errol was a strange mixture," said David Niven. "A great athlete of immense charm and evident physical beauty. He stood legs apart, arms folded and crowing lustily atop the Hollywood dung heap, but he suffered I think from a deep inferiority complex; he also bit his nails. Women loved him passionately.

"Flynn was a magnificent specimen of the rampant male – outrageously good looking!"

In 1936, now one of the world's leading personalities, Errol Flynn, who had always had a mad, almost compulsive passion for the sea – "no woman has ever been able to compete with the sea for my love" – bought a yacht and named it "Sirocco" after the boat he once co-owned back in his halcyon days in New Guinea – just a handful of years before. The yacht, like the house saw a tremendous turnover of women – all eager to get to grips with Flynn down below deck – in a very short space of time. Like its owner, the yacht's reputation as a floating passion paradise became infamous! It was here that Flynn was in total command and *in* his element, and it stayed that way for several years to come.

However, it was as a result of his so called sex escapades on board "Sirocco" that in 1942, Flynn was arrested and charged with statutory rape. He was accused of having had unlawful sex with *two* girls who were under eighteen, the legal age of consent in the State of California. One of the alleged incidents took place on dry land, with a girl called Peggy Satterlee. The other at sea, with one Betty Hansen, where during a swim and sex party, as she called it, Flynn had made love to her in front of every port hole on board the boat ... *and* kept his socks on throughout the entire proceedings!

Both girls had very dubious and colorful backgrounds and their pasts left very much to be desired. Flynn was acquitted on all charges and there was applause in the court when the verdict was read out. But the trial, which he was convinced was a "frame-up" and politically motivated, had a very lasting effect on him and some of his friends admitted that he was never quite the same, sparkling Errol Flynn again. Indeed, shortly afterwards, depression set in and he tried to commit suicide.

The rape trial did wonders for his reputation as a lady-killer, though. The world had always suspected him of being a playboy, and superstud, but had never known the truth. The trial had only helped to bring everything out into the open, and now they knew. All the rumors, all the stories of his affairs, *were* true! A new legend was created and a new catchphrase among GI's spawned. "In Like Flynn" became *the* in thing to say to describe how a person got on with his latest girl friend!

But the other side of the coin showed Flynn besieged with poison pen letters, threatening telephone calls, and a whole string of young girls demanding his money with tales of how Errol was really the father of their newly born child!

Things could never quite be the same again.

He divorced Lily Damita in 1942 and later married Norah Eddington, a young beauty he had actually met in court during the rape scandal. He was still totally dependent on his own independent life at his magnificent new bachelor home in Mulholland Drive, and set Norah up in a home of her own. Flynn's new playboy pad was the height of luxury. It was equipped with the latest electronic gadgetry which allowed one bedroom ceiling to part and reveal the open sky above. There were mirrors all over the bedroom ceilings and David Niven actually described the bedrooms as "Battlefields". There was always a stream of young nubile girls, only too ready to get a personal demonstration of all the new gadgetry and to discuss battle maneuvers with its owner.

However, Errol was drinking more by now and becoming dependent on drugs. In the end it was these excesses that caused the break up of his second marriage in 1948.

Flynn was on a one-way ticket to destruction! The booze, the birds and the drugs were by now a regular routine. A daily diet of vodka and morphine and whatever else he could get his hands on. He also suffered spasmodically from a severe form of malaria – first contracted in the New Guinea jungles – and a mild form of tuberculosis. It was amazing that he ever lasted as long as he did.

Two years after his divorce from Nora, he married a young actress named Patrice Wymore, in Monte Carlo, while on a trip to Europe. On the day of their wedding, he was accused of the statutory rape of a seventeen year old Denise Duvivier on board his brand new yacht "Zaca". He was supposed to have made love to the girl in the ship's shower room. But on inspection by an eminent French High Court judge, the shower cubicle was proved to be too small, and the act of love-making an impossibility even for the redoubtable talents of Errol Flynn. The case was thrown out of court immediately.

Not long afterwards, he walked out on his contract with Warner Brothers Pictures and left for Europe where he got involved with the disastrous movie "William Tell", for which he put up all of his savings – nearly $500,000 ... and lost the lot before half the film had even been completed. It was another of life's bitter blows, and he spent the next four years recovering, aboard his yacht and drifting like a floating "bum" from one Mediterranean port to the next. As long as the vodka didn't run out he was happy! He did make the odd film though, one in Italy, and two not very good efforts, in England.

In 1956, washed-up, broke, and almost deserted by all of his friends, he was suddenly summoned back to Hollywood to make a film called "Istanbul". This time however, he was *not* playing the sex symbol, the dashing young swashbuckler with a devil-may-care attitude. He was playing himself! He made three more films playing debauched and drunken characters – "The Sun Also Rises", "Too Much Too Soon" and "The Roots of Heaven". It was typecasting, but in these films, Errol Flynn did his best work and gave fine acting performances.

He died in Vancouver on October 14th, 1959, at the age of fifty. The official cause of death was a heart attack, though the drink, and the drugs and the sex ... had all done their bit to contribute to his demise. His body was weakened, too, by his regular bouts of malaria. He was a wreck and quite simply his body could take no more. It had already taken everything to excess.

With him at the time of his death was the young and beautiful seventeen year old actress Beverley Aadland, with whom a few months before he had made his last movie "Cuban Rebel Girls". She was his constant companion, following his separation from Patrice Wymore.

Flynn was in Vancouver at that time for one reason and one reason alone ... to escape the clinging arms of the law. Back in California, he was on the *Wanted* list once again for statutory rape!

Flynn never learned – but that was the story of his life!

3
WARREN BEATTY
...Health Freak with a diet of girls

There's a well-known saying in Hollywood circles: If it moves, wears a skirt and looks fairly attractive, Warren Beatty will ... make a play for it. (The actual phrase used, is slightly more descriptive and leaves very little to the imagination).

Another, scrawled on the wall of a well-known Los Angeles nightclub, states quite simply that he is the best lover in the world.

One newspaper described him as ''the Great Lover of Today'', and went on to say that for his exploits in the bedroom — or wherever else he does it — Warren Beatty should be awarded an Oscar. Another called him ''one of the world's most desirable men'' ... and a third — ''a dedicated hedonist''.

Even his sister Shirley MacLaine admitted — ''I'd like to do a love scene with him. I haven't seen him nude since he was six and I'd sure as hell like to find out what all the shouting is about.''

And actor/director Woody Allen put it all quietly into perspective: ''If I come back in another life, I want to be Warren Beatty's finger-tips!''

Beatty's reputation as a superstud is world famous. Indeed, he is much better known for his activities as a man-about-bed, than for any of his acting achievements, which is a great shame. He is really a very fine actor and equally good as a producer/director.

It is a fair bet that the average man in the street would be hard pressed to name any three of his pictures, yet would have no trouble at all listing half-a-dozen or so of the girls that have littered his life. Unfortunately, that, as they say, is showbusiness.

Warren Beatty's sexual conquests really do read like a cast of thousands, a fact made abundantly clear by Hollywood columnist Sheilah Graham, who wrote — ''Warren could be President if he wanted to be. He could win with the votes of the women he has loved!''

Still, "the women he has loved" haven't been entirely confined to famous actresses and celebrities, far from it. It doesn't really matter who the girl is as long as she is available. Warren is *always* available and *always* on the look out for girls and he has bestowed his sexual favors on the likes of waitresses, maids, Press agents and promotion girls, groupies and shop assistants. Anyone.

Actress Faye Dunaway, with whom he co-starred in the movie "Bonnie and Clyde" in 1967, revealed that he and actor Jack Nicholson spent many times together cruising along Hollywood's Sunset Strip — "a pair of male chauvinists, looking for a pair of broads".

And so far, none of the numerous "sextras" has complained. Far from it. ...

One of his many unknown lovers rated Warren as "the greatest lover. The best I've ever had". Another added: "He can keep going all night!"

However, it is his involvement with some of the most celebrated and successful women in the world — there have been numerous rumors about a romance between Beatty and America's former First Lady Jackie Kennedy Onassis — that have caused all the headlines and given him a label as a Red Hot Lover. It is, quite simply, a legendary list, containing Faye Dunaway, of course, Lee Radziwell, Brigitte Bardot, Liv Ullman, Jean Seberg, Candice Bergen, Maya Plisetskaya, Joni Mitchell, Dewi Sukarno, Vanessa Redgrave, Diana Ross, and Kate Jackson ... to name but a mere handful.

Elizabeth Taylor once said that on a scale of one to ten, Warren Beatty's body rated *fifteen*!

Old favorite Britt Ekland added: "Warren is the most divine lover of all. His libido was as lethal as high octane gas. I had never known such pleasure or passion in my life."

He even managed to satisfy the needs of *two* women at the same time, as Mynah Bird recalled: "We made love right there in Roman's (Polanski) bedroom at the top of the stairs. When it was over, I got up to have a bath and glanced over to the other side of the bed.

"I was amused to find that Warren had forgotten to tell me there was another girl there with us. In the excitement and the dark, I hadn't noticed."

Warren Beatty certainly has an amazing power over women. A power which once drove Natalie Wood to leave her first-time-around husband Robert Wagner, and forced Leslie Caron away from Peter Hall — who later sued for divorce citing Beatty as co-respondent. A power which left another famous celebrity "helpless. All I wanted to do was jump into bed with him!"

On another occasion a girl phoned the Los Angeles suicide prevention center, threatening to jump from a high-rise building if Warren wouldn't talk to her. Luckily, he did ... and she didn't jump.

So just what is his secret of success? What has he got that others haven't?

Well, for a start he is a multi-millionaire. He owns 40% of "Bonnie and Clyde", which has so far netted him a mere $5,000,000. He's good looking, too, in a boyish sort of way. Six foot, two inches tall, with blue eyes, (though he does need to wear glasses constantly to combat near-sightedness) and dark brown hair.

He keeps himself in shape, too, and takes vitamins. He rarely drinks — "A couple of beers and he's under the table," said his one-time girlfriend Michelle Phillips — and he never smokes, or resorts to drugs.

"He is one of the most charming men I have ever met," said Faye Dunaway, trying to find an answer. "He has a totally unconventional appeal to women. It is direct and audacious. He plays to shock — and he is boyish, which is immensely appealing. He appeals to the feminine wish to be engulfed."

The late Vivien Leigh — they made "The Roman Spring of Mrs Stone" together in 1961 — once said: "He has the kind of magnetic sensuality you could light torches with," ... while Michelle Phillips added: "Warren is a very, very attractive man. Totally charming, intelligent and ... very exciting to be with."

Kate Jackson, the one-time member of "Charlie's Angels" called him "the most amazing man." A sentiment echoed by actress Lee Grant: "Warren has a Peter Pan quality. He teaches his conquests to fly and they have extraordinary experiences with him."

And Paula Prentiss — who starred with him in "The Parallax View" in 1974: "He is absolutely gorgeous, of course. Warren is amazingly powerful, both to work with and in himself. Obviously, it's very tempting to go to bed with someone as pretty and intelligent as that."

Warren Beatty inherited his intelligence and his good looks from his school teacher father Ira Beaty — Warren added the extra "t" to the surname later in life when he was just making headway as an actor — who was a High School Principal and later became a realtor. From Kathlyn, his mother, he gained a love of drama and acting. She developed a great interest in amateur dramatics and encouraged her son (and daughter Shirley) in this direction. Kathlyn was also very much of a romantic — It must have rubbed off on her son somewhere along the line.

He was born into a Baptist family, in Richmond, Virginia, on March 30th, 1937, under the sign of Aries — The Ram. It was appropriate.

When he was quite young, the family moved to Arlington, Virginia, where he later attended the Washington and Lee High School. His childhood, he admits, was very lonely and he was very unhappy. "I felt different from the other kids — I didn't know *how* I was, but I just *knew* I was."

At High School, he learned to play piano, and spent many hours at home in the cellar, bashing out tunes on the keyboard, and singing to old Al Jolson records. It was a talent he was to use to earn money later in life. But his two great passions were for grid-iron football — he played center and later turned down several football scholarships — and amateur dramatics, which instilled into him a desire for the theater and a need to act.

He graduated from High School in 1952 at the age of fifteen and took a temporary job at Washington's National Theater as an usher, in order to get "the atmosphere of the theater", before he joined the Northwest University of Speech and Drama to train for his chosen profession. A year or so later, he studied under Stella Adler in New York. "She equipped me with a certain amount of arrogance," he often said.

Jobs for aspiring young actors, however, were hard to come by, so to pay the rent on his furnished room and supplement his income, Warren took various part-time employment, sometimes working as a laborer or bricklayer, and often appearing in a New York bar, playing piano.

Gradually, though, acting parts rolled his way. He landed a couple of appearances in television series and one-off plays, and he played in provincial theater and summer stock. Things were looking up.

Then in 1959, he got a break – many people have said it was through the influence of his sister Shirley – to appear in a Broadway play called ''A Loss of Roses''. He jumped at the chance but it ran for precisely *twenty-five performances*. Beatty came out of it all with glowing pride and some very good Press reviews which was enough to bring the ''larger boys'' of showbusiness rushing to see this new star-in-the-making. Even before the final curtain had descended on the play, Warren was preparing to go to Hollywood after signing a movie contract with MGM! He was on his way. ...

He was twenty-two when he arrived in the movie capital of the world, and he was also unknown. He started dating Jane Fonda, then a young starlet who was also trying to establish herself in films, and on one of their dates, he came face-to-face with Joan Collins, in a Los Angeles restaurant. The chemistry was instantaneous.

''He was very charming,'' said Joan. ''He could charm any woman.''

Shortly afterwards, she told a close friend that Warren ''was the best thing that ever happened to me.'' It wasn't long before they were living together.

''We became inseparable,'' she said. ''We seemed to have everything in common. We would stay up all night talking, laughing and exploring each others' bodies.

''He was insatiable. Three, four, five times a day, *everyday* was not unusual for him. I had never known anything like it.''

She also discovered that he had another unusual passion in life.

''He was never happier than when he was on the phone,'' she admitted. ''He often made twenty to thirty calls a day, and sometimes to the same person three or four times. Telephoning was secondary to his main passion which was making love – and he was also able to accept phone calls at the same time!''

24

Beatty spent two years with Joan Collins, during which time he asked her to marry him ... and they became engaged. Yet as the affair progressed, it developed into a love-hate relationship with Warren living up to his Aries tendencies for being "exceedingly possessive, terribly jealous and monstrously stubborn." Whenever Joan was away from the love nest, filming, he was convinced she was having an affair and being unfaithful. In the end, their own affair quietly ended. It hadn't been helped when she discovered she was pregnant ... and Warren forced her to have an abortion.

"I desperately wanted to keep the baby," said Joan. "But the fact that he wouldn't even consider it, hurt me dreadfully."

In 1961, Warren made his first movie, "Splendour In The Grass", with Natalie Wood. It was the start of not only a brilliant acting career, but a publicity-filled romance with the young actress that ruined her marriage to Robert Wagner. When she discovered Warren had no intentions of marrying her, she walked out of his life, completely shattered by the relationship.

French actress Leslie Caron was the next to fall under the Beatty spell and like her predecessor, she left her husband, who in turn filed for divorce, to live with Warren.

However, throughout their short affair, his wandering eyes got the better of him and he was unfaithful on many occasions. When Leslie discovered his infidelity, she, too, walked out. "I will not tolerate unfaithfulness," she said. "That's why I left Warren."

He was heartbroken. "I think a very short relationship where you tell the truth to someone is in many ways more satisfying than a long relationship where the truth becomes painful. The decision to end an affair is never mine. And it is never without considerable cost. Where sex is involved, you become very vulnerable and when separation takes place ... God, the pain. Even the promiscuous can feel pain!"

For the next few years, he drifted from one casual affair to the next, until in 1967 he met English actress Julie Christie. Everyone including his father, Ira, expected his wandering days to finally come to an end. Julie was different, and it was surely only a matter of time before they married.

Actually when they first met, Julie was totally oblivious to his advances. Beatty's old faithful stand-by — the charm — didn't work at all, and she played very hard to get. She even turned him down when he first tried to sleep with her!

Still it was Warren's total dedication to capturing Miss Christie that finally won the day. He simply wouldn't take "no" for an answer and followed her halfway around the world (from America to Europe and back) trying to win her favor. All the time, though, she rejected his advances.

In the end, she gave in under the sheer strain of Beatty's approaches, and Warren immediately admitted to being in love with the English rose. She moved into his apartment, but declined his almost daily proposals of matrimony. "We haven't lived all that differently from married people" she told the Press. "We just haven't married." Secretly Julie confided in her friends that she knew all about Beatty's reputation and *he* had to change before she would marry him. She was a one-man-woman and wanted Warren to be a one-woman-man. That certainly wasn't *his* style, for during the seven years they lived together, he was constantly straying from the fold of domestic bliss. He was up to his usual tricks in the infidelity department, and had discreet affairs on the side with Joni Mitchell, Liv Ullman and Goldie Hawn.

"When we met, he made the obligatory pass," said Goldie. "I thought he really did want to whisk me off to the bedroom. Then I realized it was just Warren. He does it with everyone. The woman who marries him will have to be non-smothering and non-clinging. The stronger she is, the better her chances of holding him."

It was amazing that his affair with Julie Christie lasted for so long. Yet it did survive and away from their love-making they even managed to make two movies together — "McCabe And Mrs. Miller" in 1971, and "Shampoo" in 1974, which his close friends agreed was a very true reflection on the life of the *real* Warren Beatty; the stud. But when Julie finally realized that her man would not be changed, she left him, just like all the others had done before. This time no amount of pleading and coaxing and chasing would make her change her mind.

Still you can't keep a good stud down for long ... in more ways than one. And after Julie Christie had come and gone, Warren turned to the former Mamas and Papas singer Michelle Phillips, who for the next three years was installed in his life as his permanent mistress. Though, he still managed to arrange the odd extra curricula affair on the quiet with anyone else he fancied or who came along.

"Warren's life is a stream of light, casual affairs," said Michelle. "And that's the way he wants it. He wants to have his cake *and* eat it, *and* burn the candle at *five* ends."

Naturally enough towards the end, their romance turned a little sour. After the break up Michelle told an English newspaper: "Warren can be boring. He could make me feel so childish and guilty for wanting to stay in bed all day eating ice cream and making love.

"His idea of a good time is five hours on the phone. He spends more time on the phone than doing anything else.

American model Candy Moore was next in line. She too, told the same newspaper about her life with the superstud. "Warren is a charmer. He just sits there and fills you up with charm. He tells you you're fantastic and so beautiful and so intelligent and the girl he's been looking for all his life.

"He does most of his chatting-up on the phone. He's crazy about it. He's very good at talking you into things and he talked me into sleeping with him.

"And he's great in bed. Very, very good, that's for sure. I wouldn't give him ten out of ten. Let's say nine and a half. He wasn't the best — Rod Stewart was."

Then came Woody Allen's former live-in fiancée Diane Keaton, who emerged as everyone's favorite choice to become the first Mrs. Beatty. She had other ideas, and after a two year romance, in which Warren proposed marriage on many occasions and actually waited a whole year for her reply — which of course was NO! — she went off with Warren's former birding-buddy and partner in pick-ups — Jack Nicholson! It's a hard life being promiscuous.

Since arriving in Hollywood in 1959, Warren Beatty has gorged himself to excess on a diet of health food, vitamins, and *girls!* Yet, unlike some of his rivals in the superstud stakes, he had always managed to remain on friendly terms with most of the girls long after their relationships have ended. Perhaps that is his secret of success!

A close friend of Warren's Bob Towne explained. "He doesn't sweet-talk women. He's very straight forward and very honest. They don't feel they have been had or seduced into anything. That's why even when they break up, there are never any recriminations. He has had a good time, but so have they!"

So there ... but what of Warren himself? He is loathe to talk about his affairs — "Not only is it in bad taste, but there are others involved, so I would be betraying their privacy as well as my own."

It was once said that he was an actor who didn't like to act, just maybe he is a superstud who doesn't like to. ...

Michelle Phillips has another view. "He says he doesn't like the Press — but he *does* like their image of him with women. And he encourages it to go on by his lifestyle. He *enjoys* his reputation."

... Which is not exactly the way he sees himself. "Look this image people have of Warren Beatty bears no reality to me. It's amazing? It's nice. But it's rubbish.

"It's a by-product of being in the public eye that people are going to say things about you. God, in fifteen years, I don't think there is anything that hasn't been said, or implied about me.

"If I tried to keep up with what was said of me sexually, I would be as Frank Sinatra once said, speaking to you from a jar in the University of Chicago Medical Center ..."

4
CLARK GABLE

...A king by any other name

Towards the end of his most famous film, "Gone With The Wind", Clark Gable as Rhett Butler turned to Scarlet O'Hara (Vivien Leigh) and uttered the immortal words (and a clarion call to male chauvinism) – "Frankly, my dear, I don't give a damn."

When it came to women, Gable quite frankly, didn't give a damn. True, he worshipped them all and regularly enjoyed them, sometimes almost to excess – writer Anita Loos once described him as having a rabbit mentality when it came to sex and she added that he had "that old, early American male idea that you take any girl that comes your way." Yet, he treated all his women just exactly how *he* wanted to treat them, and if they didn't like it, it was their hardship. He tired of their feminine wiles very quickly.

Gable's image on celluloid was exactly the same. He was a rascal and a rogue who wasn't afraid to rough the girl up a little if she got out of hand. He was the screen's first *real* male chauvinist – and the movies' first *real* macho man. He was new ... and different – and brought a breath of fresh air to the cinema which had been dominated by the dramatically contrived "Great Lovers" – Rudolph Valentino, John Gilbert and Ramon Novarro.

Clark Gable wasn't the greatest actor in the world, though what he did, he did competently enough, and he was certainly exciting, definitely exhilerating to watch ... and *all* man.

One writer, appraising his great presence on screen sometime later, wrote: "The screen Gable insinuated he had a power to give orgasms." Women simply adored him, and desired him, *and* chased after him. Clark didn't need to go hunting, for them. "I think every woman he ever met was in love with him," said actress Loretta Young.

Hedda Hopper, the queen of Hollywood columnists put it all into perspective.

"Women flocked around him like moths around a candle – duchesses, show girls, movie stars, socialites – name them he could have had them." And often *did*!

Clark Gable was a sex symbol in every sense of the word, but he was also a man's man and admired by members of his own sex for his no-nonsense yet gallant approach to his girls. He was larger than life – and they longed to emulate him. He had everything going for him and it wasn't surprising that he was the biggest male star Hollywood had ever known.

It is a well-known – and well documented – fact that Gable used women for his own ends, to get what he wanted out of life. He married his first wife Josephine Dillon in 1924 because he felt she could further his career as an actor – and to a certain degree, she did just that. He married his second wife Ria Langham seven years later, because he was convinced she could give him breeding, class and sophistication. *She* didn't do too badly, either.

Yet in his early days as an aspiring actor, women often used *him* for their own ends. Still, he didn't mind too much, he benefitted from the experiences anyway.

In 1925 when he was just breaking into the legitimate theater, he landed a minute part in a touring version of "Romeo and Juliet" starring the formidable Jane Cowl. He had actually been hand-picked for the job by Miss Cowl personally, (who was obviously more captivated by his six-foot-two physique) *not* for his acting ability, but to render another special service to *her* in the dressing room before, and often after, each performance. Clark must have been pretty good at the job, too, because he was promoted shortly afterwards, given a much more substantial part in the play *and* a ten dollar a week raise in salary!

A year later, the same thing happened again! This time, the actress concerned was Pauline Frederick who was starring in the play "Madame X". Clark auditioned for a part and was once again given a small rôle. But soon – true to form – he was playing the leading man, certainly not on stage, but definitely in Miss Frederick's affections – though legend has it that she proved too much for even the twenty-five-year-old actor to handle. He was alleged to have confided in friends: "That woman acts as though she's never going to see another man!"

It didn't take Clark Gable long to become a legend in Hollywood however, once he had arrived on the scene. He was soon hailed as the "king". He'd come along just at exactly the right moment and regularly acknowledged the fact. "The king stuff is pure bull," he said. "I eat and drink and go to the bathroom just like anybody else. I'm just a lucky slob from Ohio who happened to be in the right place at the right time and I had a lot of smart guys helping me."

Once he had come to terms with his image, he revelled in his reputation of all-American ruggedness which he openly admitted was in the main, invented by MGM publicity man Howard Strickling. Whatever else you could say about him, Clark was a good company man. He'd known too many years of poverty and hardship to go against the big Hollywood studio system, and he didn't want to go back to that. His philosophy in life was that a star was only as good as his last movie, and he lived by that code which often led to rumors about his excessive meanness. But if the company said in its publicity handouts that he was a great outdoor sportsman and hunter ... Clark hunted, and soon grew to like it! If the company said he was a great angler ... Clark was up at the crack of dawn fishing! If the company said he played golf ... Clark was out on the nearest course playing eighteen holes whenever the opportunity arose!

The whole publicity campaign was designed to create a larger than life character – and it certainly succeeded. He emerged as America's sweetheart and the screen's new and virile Great Lover. He also did wonders for the huntin', shootin', fishin', and golfin' industries in the States. Gable certainly set trends.

When he starred in the movie "It Happened One Night" in 1934, for which he won his only Academy Award, he was shown in one scene stripping down to his underclothes. When it was revealed in the shot that he wore no under shirt, audiences naturally assumed that the great man himself wore nothing under his shirt. An all-American macho man would have no time for such garments.

After the movie's release, sales of men's undershirts slumped dramatically, so much so that the American underwear manufacturers *actually* complained to the film industry that Gable's bare-chested antics were bad for their business.

Clark Gable was headline news. Wherever he went, whatever he did was reported in all the newspapers all over the world ... and, of course, rumors about his love life abounded.

When he first appeared with Jean Harlow in the film "Red Dust", it was reported that the two superstars were having an affair. In fact, almost every one of Gable's leading ladies was linked romantically with him at one time or another. So it didn't take long before another image was built up around him, that of superstud! And as each new rumor circulated, his appeal at the box office increased. Gable, too, rather liked the image, though he didn't take it too seriously.

One day while filming "It Happened One Night", he put a large hammer down the front of his trousers before grabbing co-star Claudette Colbert in a passionate embrace. When she screamed ... Clark removed the offending article, and brought the house down. Everyone on the set was doubled up with laughter.

Another time, however, he rejected a third party's offer of the services of sex Goddess Lupe Velez, because "she'll be all over town telling everybody I'm a lousy lay," he said – and that would be bad for the image. Gable prefered his women *not* to be too demanding, and not to ask too many questions ... and to keep quiet afterwards. That's why for many years he was a frequent patron of Hollywood's leading brothels and whore houses and was renowned for his one-night stands with waitresses, publicity girls, and anyone else who was convenient. Those who knew him agreed that he was no Great Lover between the sheets – indeed his third wife Carole Lombard was once heard to say – "I love Pa (her pet name for Gable; he called her Ma) but he's a lousy lay." She could well have been teasing, she was certainly renowned for her jibes. But she did once announce to a crowded Press conference in all seriousness that Clark wasn't circumcised!

Gable did, of course, have several affairs with his leading ladies. He once held up shooting on the film "The Call Of The Wild", which was on location, because he was paying far too much attention to actress Loretta Young. When the story of the hold-up in production got back to the Press, the film crew blamed the delay on bad weather.

Joan Crawford was another of Clark's leading ladies who continued to play love scenes once the camera had finished rolling. At the time of their affair, she was married to Douglas Fairbanks Junior – and the MGM publicity boys tried desperately to keep the story out of the newspapers. They didn't have much luck. The story goes that local gamblers even gave odds on the match and fully expected the affair to lead to marriage.

Crawford and Gable made two films in 1931 – "Dance Fools Dance" and "Possessed" – and throughout filming, both stars made a habit of arriving early for work each morning, and leaving much later at night. Most people assumed their affair took place in their respective dressing rooms.

Miss Crawford adored Clark Gable. She called him the sexiest man in Hollywood and said he had more "sheer animal magic than anyone in the world and every woman knew it."

William Clark Gable was born in Cadiz, Ohio, on February 1st, 1901. His father, William H. Gable was a wildcatter – a man who worked in the oil fields. He went wherever he was needed, wherever there was work, and consequently spent many days away from his home and family. Clark's mother, Adeline was frail and suffered from epilepsy. Her marriage was an unhappy one and very short. She died ten months after giving birth to her son. She was thirty-one.

Because of his father's wanderlust, Clark was brought up by his grandparents for the next eighteen months, until Will H. married – for the second time – a young hat-maker called Jennie Dunlap whom he called "all woman". The family moved to Hopedale, Ohio, where Will bought some land.

The young William Clark had a normal upbringing and childhood. He admitted to being spoiled by Jennie, and was constantly fighting with his father.

He wasn't the greatest scholar in the world – far from it – but he tried hard and that was the main thing. He did excel at baseball, however, and made the school team. He could also play the French horn and appeared regularly with the town band. Playing in the band gave the young boy the chance to appear before large audiences – and he revelled in the experience, and liked being the center of attraction. He was thirteen.

Three years later, father Will decided to quit the oil wells – for the time being at least – and bought a small farm, sixty miles from town in a place called Ravenna. Clark, now a strapping lad of sixteen, was expected to leave school and help his father run the farm. He hated the whole idea. "I just wasn't cut out to be a farmer," he once told a journalist. So he decided to leave home and head back to Hopedale where he got a job working for a mine crew. A few months later, he moved to Akron, where he was employed in the time-keeping department of a rubber tyre company, and it was here, that he discovered movies for the first time, *and* "live" theater. Needless to say, he was captivated by the glamor of it all, and in his spare time, he worked at the Akron Music Hall as a call boy. It didn't bother him at all that the job paid no money. He was happy enough being in the theater and near to actors. At one time he was even given a walk-on part in one of the theater's productions. It was an experience he never forgot, and one which was to shape his career, for now he had finally found his true vocation in life. He *had* to act, nothing else mattered. He was eighteen.

That same year, Jennie, his stepmother, died, and his father decided to sell the farm and move back into the oil fields, this time in Oklahoma. Clark, unable to make much headway in his acting career, later joined him … and spent the next three years regretting the fact.

At twenty-one, however, he inherited $300 from his grandfather and decided there and then to try his luck once again as an actor, though his father tried desperately to make him change his mind, but with no success. Father and son didn't speak for the next ten years.

With money in his pocket Clark set out to establish himself in the acting profession. Initially, he returned to Akron to find his acting colleagues and friends but was told that they had all moved on to Kansas City. So he hastily followed and got a job in a touring tent show. When that folded, he became a lumberjack, and later still, used his skill as an actor to charm customers into buying the ties he sold in a department store in Portland, Oregon. However, he did manage to join a local amateur theater group, and later worked for the Astoria Players Stock Company where he met his first real girlfriend, Franz Dorfler, and they later became engaged. Up until then, friends recalled that Clark hadn't shown the slightest interest in women.

In the summer of 1923, Broadway actress Josephine Dillon arrived in Portland to start a theater group, and one of her first students was Clark Gable. He soon became her protegé.

Josephine taught the eager-to-learn young actor many things. How to develop expressions, and how to lower his rather high-pitched, whining voice and control it into a much more masculine and seductive growl. She also made him change his name to *Clark Gable*. Up until then, he had billed himself in various ways — W. C. Gable, William C. Gable, or Billy Gable, whatever took his fancy.

A year later, when she moved to Hollywood, Gable followed her ... and a few months after, in December 1924, they were married. She was forty, he a mere twenty-three. It didn't matter, Clark had married her to fire his own ambition. Josephine was the first person of any note, to tell him he had talent, and he believed she could develop that talent and make him into a star. She, for her part, helped him to land acting jobs as an extra in a number of silent movies, but he spent much of his early career on the stage in touring theater companies, one of which was run by Lionel Barrymore who later got him his first Hollywood contract at MGM. Barrymore was quite impressed with his acting talent, but told him to get more experience.

Throughout his marriage to Josephine Dillon, Clark had great difficulty remaining faithful. He didn't even try. If a woman was available and in the right place at just the right time, *and* made a play for *him*, he wouldn't let her down. If he could profit from the affair, so much the better. Clark was very single minded.

One of his touring theater companies took him to Houston, Texas, where he soon established himself through his acting, as the town's resident and personal heart-throb. The Gable magic was beginning to work at last. Young girls swooned when they saw him on the street (these were the 1920's after all when swooning was all the rage); older women paid him far more attention, particularly late at night in his dressing room.

It was in Houston that he met the wealthy Texas society lady Ria Langham — who was destined to become the second Mrs. Gable. She found him charming, and irresistible and followed him to New York where he enjoyed a fair success on Broadway in the play "Machinal". During the rehearsals for the play he told Josephine he wanted nothing more to do with her. She had served her purpose in his life.

For the next two years, Clark toured America in various plays including "The Last

Mile'', which was destined to take him to Hollywood and to the attention of the movie makers. He made his first major film ''The Painted Desert'' in 1931 for Pathé, before signing a lengthy contract with MGM. The same year he divorced Josephine Dillon and married Ria. Like the first Mrs. Gable, his second wife was seventeen years his senior.

The movie star the world had been waiting for, had arrived ... and was raring to go.

Clark Gable became the world's most desirable man throughout the 1930's. Women literally threw themselves at him. When they found out where he was living in Hollywood, they gathered in their hundreds outside his home, waiting for a glimpse of that famous face and those large ears. In New York, when he once made a personal appearance at the Capital Theater, women of all ages stood outside the building weeping. Some were crying because they hadn't managed to see their idol, others were crying because they had. Gable was like that ... he drove women to tears!

He had a terrific power over women and not surprisingly he had many casual romances, notably with Joan Crawford, Loretta Young, English actress Elizabeth Allen, society girl Mary Taylor and many more. There were always agents and managers, and Public Relations executives only too willing to offer the services of their glamorous starlets to Gable; it was one of the perks of the job. Clark never complained.

Yet although he was very discreet about these illicit affairs – and the studio certainly helped in covering up any scandal that involved their major investment – news still got back to Ria and put a tremendous strain on their marriage. It was inevitable, however, that they would separate and it was only a matter of time. The time came in 1935 when Clark started believing in his own publicity.

A year later he met the only woman he ever really loved according to friends – the blonde and bubbling comedy actress Carole Lombard. They were instantly attracted to each other. He adored the way she talked, spicing each sentence with a string of the foulest four-letter words imaginable and the most obscene phrases. She could also drink and play cards ... and Clark loved her for it. Above all else, she had the ability to make Gable laugh.

Their affair was the talk of Hollywood and much further afield, too. After all, Clark Gable was one of the biggest movie stars in the history of the movies. Carole was an ideal partner, she did everything to please him. She went hunting with him, played golf with him ... and he loved her even more.

On one occasion, when they were away hunting, the morning fog was so low that it was impossible to shoot the ducks and geese that were flying overhead. They couldn't see them! Gable was prepared to sit and wait for the blanket to clear and the air to clear, but not Carole: ''I can think of something better to do,'' she said. So they climbed back into their tiny duck-hide and made love until the fog lifted.

They married in 1939 after Ria had finally consented to a divorce: it cost Gable $286,000, paid over three years in settlement. They bought a ranch and settled down. It looked like the perfect Hollywood marriage.

It was the same year, that he made the memorable ''Gone With The Wind'' and just twelve months after he officially became the ''King'' of Hollywood.

The ''King'' idea was supposedly thought up by Ed Sullivan, who ran a competition in a syndicated newspaper group asking his readers to vote for the stars they thought were ''King'' and ''Queen'' of Hollywood. Gable was the unanimous choice for the male award; Myrna Loy became his ''Queen''. Over twenty million people voted!

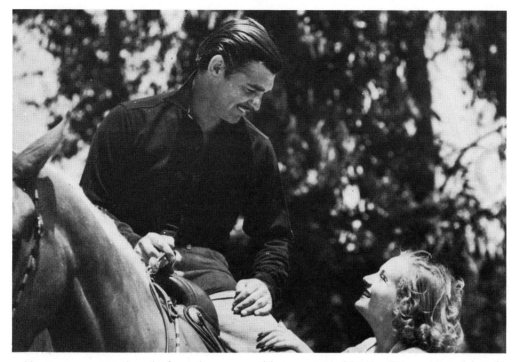

However, some time before the competition appeared in the Press, legend has it that Spencer Tracy dubbed Gable as "King". They were working on the movie "Test Pilot" together, when one morning Tracy arrived early on the set only to find his co-star surrounded by girl autograph hunters. Clark was revelling in the situation, lauding it, as Spencer later reported. He leapt out of his car and shouted "Hail to the King". The title stuck!

Gable's marriage to Carole Lombard was exceedingly happy, yet he still played the field whenever he had the opportunity. He liked a little bit on the side, and took every opportunity that came his way. During the filming of "Gone With The Wind", he was regularly making love to one of the many starlets who had small roles in the movie and there were also many rumors about an affair with Lana Turner. Nothing was ever proved and Lana Turner herself denied it. "Ours was a closeness without intimacy, we never had an affair," she said later.

However, his marriage to Carole Lombard was tragically short. On January 12th, 1942, — with the United States now fully committed to a war with Germany and Japan, and all the Hollywood stars doing their "bit" for the war effort — Carole set out on a Government sponsored tour of major US cities to sell War Bonds. Four days later, the plane on which she was returning home to Hollywood, ran into a storm and crashed into the Nevada mountains near Las Vegas. There were no survivors.

Gable never fully recovered from the blow.

In August of the same year, he joined the US Army-Airforce as a Private, asked for no special privileges and got none. A few months later, he graduated as an officer, but it was tough going. He later served with the 351st Bomber Group in England and flew on several dangerous bombing missions, for which he was awarded the Distinguished

Flying Cross and the Air Medal, and he became the hero he so often portrayed in films. At one time, Hitler even put a price on his head of $5,000, instant promotion and a two week leave, for anyone who could capture the daring film star!

It was during his war service, however, that it was discovered Clark Gable had a fetish for cleanliness! He couldn't stand *dirt*!, and told his fellow servicemen that the reason he never took a bath was because he didn't like being surrounded by dirty water! He always preferred to take a shower. He also shaved every single hair from his body – apart from his head. Body hair, he reasoned could be contaminated by perspiration and harbored odor. He also very rarely went out with brunettes or dark haired women, because the color of their hair made them look dirty, or so he thought!

Gable's servicemen colleagues were also amazed at his tastes in women at this period in time. He preferred plain, homely and sometimes downright ugly girls, to any of the stunning lookers that would normally be associated with the most desirable man in the world. But that was Clark – always after *convenient* sex!

When he came home from war, Gable was a changed man. He started drinking heavily and in 1945 his alcoholic habits very nearly led to his death. He was driving home at dead of night after one typical heavy drinking session, when his car skidded out of control and crashed into a tree. Fortunately for Clark, the tree was on the lawn of Harry Friedman, himself a Hollywood agent and very familiar with the ground rules of the movie business. Instead of calling the police, he telephoned MGM studios who immediately went into action. Gable was patched up by a sympathetic and discreet doctor, while all visual trace of the accident was eradicated, before anyone was any wiser. The "King's" image was still intact.

Although Clark Gable might have had a little problem with liquor, when it came to women, he still reigned supreme. He was now a most eligible bachelor and had an entourage of women around him who were all eager to please. They became known as the "Gable set". There was actress Virginia Grey, cover girl Anita Colby – who actually turned down his proposal of marriage – Dolly O'Brien (another of the no-takers in the marriage stakes), Betty Chisholm, oil-millionairess Millicent Rogers, the ever-faithful actress Kay Williams and Ida Lupino. And of course, the local whore-house was always on tap when he needed a change of scenery.

But in 1949, he astounded everyone by marrying for the fourth time. His new bride was Sylvia Ashley who was formerly married to Douglas Fairbanks Senior.

It was another short-lived affair. "I've had every kind of woman. Now I have married a siren," said Clark. Their marriage lasted two years, though friends were convinced that Gable was drunk when he proposed and it was all a terrible and very costly mistake! He paid out nearly $400,000 in alimony!

He married again in 1955 after several romances including one with French model Suzanne Dadolle. It was also suggested in the Press that he was having an affair with Grace Kelly, who was regularly seen in his company after they made the film "Mogambo" together in 1953. When their liaison came to an end she told reporters that it was the difference in their ages that had brought about the split!

Clark's fifth wife was one of the former Gable set, Kay Williams who was almost a carbon copy of Lombard. On first meeting a few years before, Clark told her – "why don't you go upstairs and get undressed?" Kay's reply was for him to do something with his hat that doesn't bear thinking about! He liked a girl with spirit and from that moment onwards they got on very well together.

It was a good marriage, too. Like Lombard, Kay Williams doted on Clark. She went with him on hunting and shooting expeditions, and played golf as well. They looked good together. But it lasted just five years.

On November 5th, 1960, a day after completing his final movie "The Misfits" with Marilyn Monroe, Gable had a heart attack and was rushed to hospital. Eleven days later, the "King" died. But the legend lived on. Four months after his death, his only child – John – was born.

Clark Gable made 67 films in thirty years in Hollywood and through them he made millions of women all over the world happy. To them he was a superstar, and by the very parts he played, he was entitled to be a superstud, too. He was the all-American macho man, who just *had* to be good with girls. Yet, there were rumors, that like so many of the so-called lady-killers, Gable was impotent! It was just the price of being famous, as one of his close friends said, reacting to the slurs on Gable's masculinity. But there were literally hundreds of women who would willingly have testified to the state of his potency.

Clark Gable wasn't the most handsome of men. His ears were far too large and stuck out, which resulted in Howard Hughes once saying that he looked like a taxicab with both doors open. And he was always self-conscious of his large and cumbersome hands. He also wore dentures which were ill-fitting and caused his breath to smell terribly as Vivien Leigh, his co-star in "Gone With The Wind" found out to her utter disgust. But he certainly had "something" that drove women wild ...

Several years after his death, one of his former lovers Joan Crawford appeared on David Frost's American Television show and was asked who she thought was the most exciting man in Hollywood. She had no hesitation in naming Gable! When Frost pressed his point and asked for her reasons, the actress's reply was bleeped off the air.

"Because he had balls!" she said.

5
BURT REYNOLDS
...The All-American superstud

Burt Reynolds is *not* a man to mince his words. And when he claims – with just a hint of a glint in his eye – that he has had more women that any other man alive ... you'd better believe him! After all, it is not an idle boast that can be disproved easily, and as yet no-one has come forward to challenge him.

Still, it's easy to see why he qualifies as a "lady-killer". Burt has all the right credentials, in all the right departments even if you overlook the fact that he has worn "lifts" in his shoes on several occasions to make him look taller *and* has recently discarded his toupée in favor of a hair transplant. He is a very eligible bachelor and a millionaire movie star with more than his fair share of assets in the good looks league. So with that kind of collateral, he can surely play the field when it comes to women and have *almost* any female he takes a fancy to.

However, unlike many of his contemporaries, Burt Reynolds is not at all choosey about his women, which just might go some of the way to accounting for the many sexual conquests he talks about. As long as they are available ...

"Women are my drugs and alcohol," he has said on many occasions. "I admit I like women a lot. Young. Old. Plain. Pretty. Any women – I don't mind. Though, I'm no good with swingers. I don't like what they do or what they represent ..." which roughly translated means that he must have sampled the merchandise at least once in the past to know that he doesn't like it.

"Quite honestly," he added, "I think that most men don't really like women. They'd rather talk and tell jokes and play pool and drink beer ... with another man. And then go home to bed with their girlfriend or their wife. But I've always found that if you have the right kind of relationship, you can have all those things with a woman."

In a career that started in movies in 1961, Burt – who admits to being a flirt – has established himself as one of the world's leading sex-symbols — and if we are to believe him (and there's no reason to doubt his words), *World Champion Superstud!* However, he has yet to register his claim with the Guinness Book of Records. He has been described in the world's Press as "Mr. Sex", as "The Best Body In The World" and as "The Smoothest Woman Chaser In The Business". It is an image of which he is secretly very proud, though publicly he decries it.

"I'm not at all enamored with that kind of image — and I don't have much regard for the kind of person I've been made out to be ... a movie star swinger who tells the girl to be dressed and outta here by 5.00 a.m.

"You can only hold your stomach in for so long!

"Being in the public eye in any way is painful. Being a personality is painful. You can never give the public enough. They always want more."

However, he does take total advantage of his image and reputation. He loves all the attention he gets, despite what he might say, and uses it all to his own ends.

He told a writer: "It doesn't bother me at all to read that I'm out with a different woman every night. I'm flattered. Sometimes seeing my name in print with a gal actually gives me an excuse to meet her." And: "The other night I nearly killed myself trying to live up to a typographical error. It's amazing how much a *three* looks like an *eight*!"

The Burt Reynolds sense of humor is renowned in Hollywood and much further afield, too — and he has certainly needed to have one following some of the reviews his pictures have received from the critics. Still, although his movies have been panned unmercifully — well, most of them anyway — by the Press, Super-Burt has developed a superb talent for pulling in the punters to see his performances on the big screen. Each year, since 1973, he has been named as one of the Top Ten money-spinning box-office stars and in 1978, he was the world's top box-office attraction. He has also cultivated a superb talent for pulling in the ladies to help his performances beneath the silk screens and bed linen.

It was in 1966, just after his divorce from English actress Judy Carne, that Burt emerged in the superstud stakes, and he admitted that after leaving Judy, he embarked on a pre-meditated sexual binge — pursuing anything and everything that was available. "I woke up one morning in bed and had no idea who I was with."

Over the next few years, his name was seldom out of the papers and he was romantically linked with many of the world's most eligible women.

There was Japanese actress Miko Mayama, who cost him over two hundred dollars a week in "palimony" when their affair came to an end. Lucie Arnaz, daughter of Lucille Ball, was another to fall under the magic Reynolds' spell though their relationship came to a full stop when he started playing more than tennis with Chris Evert — who incidentally still refers to him as "such a gentleman".

Actress Catherine Deneuve was another conquest, and he very nearly married one-time Charlie's Angel Farrah Fawcett, even before she had Major-ed!

"Looking back," he said, "I was crazy not to marry Farrah. I waited too long, and a friend of mine named Lee Majors won her as his wife."

Country singer Tammy Wynette — another brief encounter — never believed he would marry again. "I don't think Burt ever secretly considers marrying again, despite what he might say. He's the kind of guy who would stop on his way down the aisle to say hello to a pretty girl in the congregation."

Still that didn't deter the long line of beauties who beat a pathway to his door ... and in rapid succession, Burt was reported to have squired actress Lori Nelson, Susan Clark, Liza Minelli, Greta Baldwin, Candice Bergen ... and many more. Quite honestly, the list was endless.

Jill Clayburgh, who co-starred with him in the movie "Starting Over" and indeed was nominated for an Academy Award for her part in the film, had a passionate affair with him several years ago. She told a newspaper that Burt had left her with one of his famous "I'll call you" lines. She added: "He never did!"

The Burt Reynolds saga started in Waycross, Georgia on February 11th, 1936. He was christened Burt after his father — who was half-Cherokee Indian and also just happened to be a local Police officer — but was known as Buddy to avoid any confusion. Yet, to confuse matters further, as far as his origins went, Burt's mother was of *Italian* extraction.

The family later moved to Riviera Beach in Florida where Burt's father became the Chief of Police at West Palm Beach. It was here that the youngster got a mean reputation for being a rebel-rouser. He was restless and resentful and had a big chip on his shoulder, something he took with him into his movie career some years later. He did, however, have one great talent at that time — for gridiron football. Though, for the early few years of his life, the only talent that was regularly on display was his ability to fight! He was always getting into scraps, but it wasn't surprising. The other neighborhood kids took great delight in taunting him mercilessly with jibes about his working class background and, worst of all, his family origins. Because of his Indian blood, he was called "Half-breed" by his so-called friends and Burt rarely turned the other cheek. If it was a fight they wanted, it was a fight they got. He seldom came away losing.

In 1951, when he had just turned fifteen, Buddy ran away from home to seek his fame and fortune. Actually, he'd simply had enough.

He got as far as South Carolina before he was arrested on a vagrancy charge and sentenced to work on the chain gang. However, he was later sent back home to Florida where he returned to Palm Beach High School and distinguished himself as a football player.

It was at about this time, too, that Burt went out with his first girlfriend — "I was attracted to her body," he smiled matter-of-fact. "Because I came from a working class family, her parents didn't approve of me and I had to use the side door when I picked her up for a date. I never forgot that."

What the girl didn't know at the time was that she was *the first* of a whole procession of females who were to invade the Reynolds private life. "Chicks who would make your eyes pop!" he once called them. There were college girls, secretaries, air hostesses, stars and starlets, singers and dancers. They all had three things in common: they were independent, they had a sense of humor, and above all else, they were available.

Even then, his reputation as a womanizer was growing, but his early sexual talents weren't quite on a par with his achievements as a football star. He performed brilliantly on the field and was signed up by the Baltimore Colts ... a professional career looked a certainty.

One Christmas Eve, though, tragedy put paid to that idea!

Burt was a bit of a reckless driver on the quiet, despite the fact that his father was a policeman. On this particular night he was driving home, a little faster than usual, when his car was involved in a terrifying collision with a truck. On impact, the roof of Burt's car was sliced away, and he was trapped in the wreckage for nearly eight hours before he was finally cut free and rushed to hospital suffering from shattered knees and a ruptured spleen. It was touch and go ...

Burt survived but he never effectively played football again.

Reynolds was devastated, and when at last he recovered, at least physically, from the accident, he decided to leave Florida and hitch-hiked to New York. He didn't stay too long in the Big Apple before returning home where he hoped he could re-establish himself as a football player. His knees had other ideas and gave out on him. So Burt was back on the road to disaster, and back on the road to New York where this time the visit lasted a little longer. However, he was continually looking at life through the bottom of an upturned bottle of alcohol — "I was well on the way to becoming a bum!"

For some reason — known to only himself — Burt started to keep company with actors in Greenwich Village and such was the impact and affect they had upon the very impressionable young man, that he soon had an urge to act himself. So, it was back to Florida to enrol in Palm Beach College to study drama. He admits to having been bitten by the acting "bug".

In 1958, Burt won the Florida Drama Award and a scholarship to attend the Hyde Park Playhouse in of all places — New York. A year later, after playing odd roles here and there on the New York stage, coupled with a few appearances on television, he

left the East coast for Los Angeles — "When all the agents went West, so did I."

He was a budding young actor now, Hollywood was at his feet ... and it was in the movie capital of the world, that he started to build the foundations of a career. He appeared extensively on television, enjoying moderate success in the long-running series "Riverboat" and "Pony Express", though he resented playing the eternal half-breed his looks gave him. He was out of work more often than not and with spare time on his hands, he spent many hours in down and out bars on skid row ... drinking too much. His working class background wouldn't lie down and the chip on his shoulder, that was nurtured in Riviera Beach, just wouldn't go away. He also retained his amazing ability at being able to pick fights whenever he wanted. Anyone who so much as dared to look at him for more than a brief moment was in trouble.

"I'd drive down to skid row, walk into a bar, wait for the inevitable crack, belt the guy in the teeth — and then go home feeling much better," Burt once told a magazine. It was almost a daily event in his life. When he didn't work as an actor, he punctuated his bouts of boozing and boxing, employed as a stunt man. After all he needed to keep fit for his sessions of more sexual matters. For by now, he was weening his reputation as a superstud.

In 1962, Burt started a two-and-a-half year stint in the long-running and highly successful TV series "Gunsmoke" — and this time he didn't seem to mind his "half-breed" role. He was on his way at last ...

It was the same year, that he met and started living with Judy Carne. In 1963, they married in a glittering publicity-packed ceremony. But three years later the marriage was at an end ... in a blaze of publicity.

"I was surprised that marriage wasn't a happy life in a rose covered cottage," said Burt. "It turns out that my wife's entire past was a life I didn't know about.

"The divorce was my fault ... my loss. Judy's a terrific person ... we had something special together."

They did indeed, for it was Judy Carne who managed to curb Burt's vicious temper and his arrogant attitude towards life. She managed to erase some of the chip from his shoulder, but *that* was hard work. And she also showed him how to settle his arguments peaceably *without* using his fists!

Their divorce in 1966 left Reynolds "devastated" for a while. But once he got over his grief, he was off on his sexual travels once more — only this time with no intention of getting hooked again. He had had three years of marriage and he needed to get *that* out of his system. He had a lot of catching up to do.

Within a very short space of time, though, he had won more rave reviews for his antics in the bedroom than any of his antics as an actor. His superstud image was slowly gaining momentum.

Six years later, two things happened that were to have a major bearing on Burt Reynolds' life.

He gave a brilliant performance in the powerful movie "Deliverance" which was to take him in to the superstar actor category and to the upper echelons of the box-office ratings.

He also started a much publicized affair with singer Dinah Shore.

Burt met Dinah Shore — who was seventeen years his senior — when he appeared on her television show. For some time now, he had been doing the rounds of the TV talk programs, laying bare his soul, in an effort to establish himself as a personality in his own right. Up until then, most newspapers had looked upon Burt as a wine drinking, woman chasing, TV actor who had had little success in "proper" movies. He resented the tag.

"I made a pact with her right at the beginning," he told a journalist. "We would just make the best of it as long as it lasted. Be honest with each other for as long as it lasted. If that was forever, terrific ... if not, we didn't want to hurt each other."

Burt spent four publicity-filled years with Dinah Shore. They were totally open about their relationship and the age difference didn't bother them at all, though it did raise a few eyebrows elsewhere. But what is more important, the liaison did no harm whatsoever to either of their careers. That was to come, for Reynolds anyway, just a few months later on in an incident that shook him rigid.

He was working on the movie "The Man Who Loved Cat Dancing" with English actress Sarah Miles. And although it was hinted at by every major international newspaper, when they were seen together, that Burt and Sarah were having an affair, nothing was ever proved! Both vehemently denied the rumors.

But they didn't stop, in fact the scandalmongers increased the pressures to find the true story, and alleged all manner of things in print.

The rumors became unbearable when Burt and Sarah were involved in the tragic and bizarre death of the actress's business manager and former love, David Whiting.

The film was being shot on location in Arizona when Whiting began to believe all the things he read in the papers about the two stars. Naturally, he assumed like many other people, they *were* having an affair.

One evening after filming, Whiting challenged Miss Miles about the rumors and, not satisfied with her answers, started knocking her about. At the inquest, it was later revealed that Sarah had returned to her room after spending a long time in Burt Reynolds' bedroom, where he was taking a massage.

It was natural for the English actress to call for help when Whiting started to slap her face. She called for Burt Reynolds. But by the time he had come to the aid of the damsel in distress, Whiting had fled the room. Sometime later he was found dead.

The Press went to town. Rumors sizzled around the world. Assumptions. Innuendo ... the news pages were alive with the story and suggestions that maybe Burt had actually fought with the dead man in defence of the fair Sarah. They were not quelled completely when the autopsy revealed that David Whiting had died from a drugs overdose.

After that incident Burt was totally shattered. "Emotionally and physically I just collapsed," he said. But for Dinah Shore who offered him perfect solace and comfort, he might not have pulled through.

He stayed with her until 1976 and then the affair petered out, with no hard feelings all round and even the Press played down the break up. Burt's itchy feet were playing him up again and he needed a change of scenery.

"After a period of time I can't go on any further. I try but I can't ... It's just that I wasn't meant to be with one person for the rest of my life."

Looking back on the romance, Burt told journalists: "If I have any class at all it is all due to Dinah Shore. She is the happiest person I know — and the classiest. She is still my best friend and very special to me."

Miss Shore would only mumble: "What Burt and I had going for us was an indoor sport."

It was after the break up of one romance that Burt turned to another and focused his attention on the Oscar-winning actress Sally Field with whom he co-starred in "Smokey And The Bandit" – the movie that made him a millionaire. It was another long-running four year affair and throughout it, Burt insisted on living by himself in his luxury Bel Air Mansion. Sally lived down the road apiece with her sons Peter and Eli in her own home. "I'm old fashioned about that," said Burt. "I wanted the kids to have some kind of values ... I didn't want them to think of me as the guy who moved in with their mother."

The sometimes temperamental, sometimes arrogant superstar was at last mellowing and there were many rumors about an imminent marriage. Still, Tammy Wynette was later proved to be right.

However, during the affiliation, Burt admitted: "My idea of a good time with a woman is to hole up for three days, watch old movies, make pizza, be silly, act like children and get the giggles".

But, maybe he said that on impulse. He certainly seems to do a lot of things like that.

Back in 1972 after topping box-office ratings for "Deliverance", he decided to take his entire career in his hand – and one or two other things as well – and pose naked for the center-fold spread of *Cosmopolitan* magazine. If he did it as an exercise in the art of publicity, he passed with flying colors ... for many months afterwards, he was the talk of the world – well, a certain part of him was anyway. It was a totally unexpected move for a superstar to make, though the exposure he gained, in more ways than one, was fantastic. Needless to say every issue of the magazine was sold out and became collectors' items.

"It was all a joke," said Burt at the time. "I felt it would be a kick. I did it to satirize *Playboy* and all the other center-folds. I felt I had the sense of humor to bring it off after the magazine came out. I was fully prepared to get into an elevator with a bunch of guys and either have to be funny, or fight my way out. But men seem to recognize it faster than women. Of course, there are always guys who love to show off by calling you a movie star faggot, but most guys just laugh and kid me about it."

His career didn't suffer at all ... on the contrary, it blossomed.

Shortly afterwards, Burt had lunch with Paul Newman and a fan came up to the two superstars and asked if Newman would mind removing his dark glasses so she could get a better view of his "gorgeous blue eyes". Burt Reynolds smiled – "You're very lucky it's only your eyes ... you should hear what they ask to see of mine!"

6
ROD STEWART
...Blondes certainly do have more fun

The lights dim. The curtains part – and the night is filled with rock 'n' roll.

A pair of high-powered spotlights straffe the stage to pick out the tall, lean figure of the man they call the most exciting singer in rock music.

For Rod Stewart, another concert – another short love affair with his doting audience – is about to begin ...

He's on stage for over two hours, arrogantly strutting about his domain like a bantam fighting cockerel – his blond coxcomb hair glistening in the ferocious lights, his brilliantly interpretive voice rasping out songs of love and sex and rock 'n' roll ...

"Do You Think I'm Sexy?", "Tonight's The Night", "The First Cut Is The Deepest", "It's All Over Now".

This is Rod's territory where every movement – a microphone stand upturned and raised to the sky in a sexual salute; a wiggle of the sleak backside that one English newspaper hailed as "the sexiest bum in rock" – is calculated to drive his fans to a frenzy!

It is here that he reigns supreme, where he has won his spurs as a superstar and super-showman ... and where everything he does is stamped with style.

Yet away from the arc lights, the razzle dazzle and the pulsating beat, Rod Stewart has an even bigger reputation to live up to ... that of lover supreme and superstud. And he has done very nicely thank you very much.

Over the years, Rod's sexploits under the blankets (or duvets if you prefer) have won him more headlines in the world's newspapers than Gold, Silver and even Platinum Discs. When it was announced that he just happened to prefer wearing ladies' silk knickers next to his own delicate skin instead of the normal manly Y-fronts, Rod received blanket coverage. Still, he knows a thing or three about blankets, especially from the underside!

47

His sexual appetite though is renowned and his diet has always included a very liberal sprinkling of long-haired blondes, with "good boobs" – he can never resist a nice pair – and long, slim legs that "go all the way up." To bend the title of one of his hit records, blondes certainly do have more fun, particularly with Rod. His list of conquests in the bedroom stakes reads like a United Nations of models and actresses – all young (well, with one or two exceptions!) and all very much available. There were English girls Dee Harrington, Sabrina Guinness, Susan George. Scandinavia's Britt Ekland. Americans Alana Hamilton (now Mrs. Rod Stewart), Liz Treadwell, Marcy Hanson, Bebe Buell ... and a few more, of various origins, thrown in for good measure.

Stewart's lust for life, or life of lust if you prefer, started in London, England, on January 10th, 1945. His parents ran a small shop in the North London suburb of Holloway, which sold newspapers, magazines, sweets, tobacco and all manner of other goodies.

When he left school, he had no musical ambitions whatsoever, in fact he was totally obsessed with playing soccer, and he didn't care for very much else. Yet, for the time being at least, he had to earn a living. So in a very short space of time he had a series of mundane jobs which included grave-digging, fence erecting, and message running. Then, when he realized he was getting absolutely nowhere, he decided to take his father's advice, and signed on with Brentford Football Club as an apprentice professional player. It was, however, a very brief apprenticeship. Faced with the prospect of having to clean the boots of his contemporaries and to "muck out" the changing rooms daily, Rod quit, turned beatnick and set out in search of sun and sea and sand and something else in Spain and Italy. He spent most of his time banning the bomb and hitching along the shores of the Mediterranean.

In 1963, he came back to England and turned to singing for a living, and joined his first group. Then began one of the most spectacular careers in international music which has taken him in and out of *most* of the world's available Hit Parades, and *some* of the world's most available bedrooms!

Rod's obsession with sex started when he was in his early teens and it has continued very healthily ever since.

He once told an English journalist that since he was a mere sixteen years old, he had never gone without sex for more than a week. The reporter just happened to be female, and maybe that particular week was almost up and Super-Rod had yet to fulfil his quota. But no matter – for Mr. Stewart added that in a twenty-five week period in England once, he dated a different woman every single night. However, he didn't elaborate on how many had breakfast with him the morning after.

Before his much publicized marriage to Alana Hamilton, he readily told an eagerly awaiting world: "I can never be faithful – maybe for an hour or two – but a lasting relationship for a rock 'n' roller ... is almost impossible!"

It was a point he proved time and time again, *even* when he was supposed to be living happily-ever-after with whichever girl friend was the flavor of that particular month.

He spent five years with model Dee Harrington, yet during all that time, Rod was forever going off the rails.

"One of his favorite pastimes was 'girl spotting' in the morning newspapers," she said. "When he saw one he liked the look of, he got his publicity agent to ring her up and invite her out to dinner. Then it was up to Rod. What happened after dinner is anyone's guess ...

"Actually, Rod was basically a very shy person. He was very aware of the fact that he was *Rod Stewart*, superstar and millionaire, and because of that he found it very awkward to chat up girls. Still, he had others to do it for him – *and* they did it all the time."

The publicity agent in question was Tony Toon who doubled up as Rod's chatter-upper-in-chief. He admitted in a wild newspaper exposure that Rod once carried on affairs with two different girls at the same time in the same town. And it was also a common event for Stewart to wave "goodbye" to one girl friend at an airport departure gate, only to rush across the terminal to greet another at the arrival desk a few minutes later.

One such event happened in San Antonio Airport in Texas. Britt Ekland was flying out after spending a few days with Rod, who was mid-way through a tough American tour, and she very nearly came face to face with her arch-rival Bebe Buell, who just happened to be flying in on the self-same mission.

The American model was forever flying in from somewhere or another to spend a few days with Rod; according to many of Stewart's close friends, she was only too willing to drop anything and everything to answer his calls. She even spent one Christmas with him in England, shacked up in a house in Surrey. Little did she realize, however, that while he was away from the house on "business", he was nipping backwards and forwards into central London to service Mercy Hanson, conveniently entrenched in a five star hotel suite. When Bebe later found out about the affair, after it was revealed in the newspapers – she hit the roof and probably Mr. Stewart as well.

Rod Stewart's most famous and certainly most written-about liaison, however, was with Swedish sexpot Britt Ekland. It was a live-in, love-in affair that was seldom out of the world's newspapers during its run of over two years. When the happy couple who by then were decidedly unhappy, split up, the Press had a field day. Miss Ekland didn't fare too badly either, selling her steamy reminiscences to anyone with enough money, and writing her memoirs which up to then was a thing only battle-scarred and weary old campaigners had done.

She then decided to take her ex-lover to court, demanding a staggering twelve million dollars in what has become known as "palimony", though both parties arrived at an amicable solution and settled out of court.

Rod first met Britt in Los Angeles in 1975 and at first, knowing his reputation as a Casanova, she played very hard to get. She even refused his amorous advances on their first date, and very few people ever turned Rod down flat! As it was, though, within a matter of weeks they were living together in Beverley Hills.

At the time of their budding romance, Rod had been living with Dee Harrington and everyone associated with the singer was in no doubt that the Britt thing was a passing fad ... and that Rod would still continue to share his home and his favors with the English model. He'll tire with Britt very soon, they hinted, yet it wasn't to be ... and Dee brought it upon herself entirely.

She caught Rod and Britt out together one night in Los Angeles, when Stewart had assured her he was attending a very important business meeting. She confronted him in no uncertain terms in the middle of the road in the middle of the night, outside an

LA nightclub. It wasn't a pretty sight. ...

People who know Rod Stewart well, will tell you that he can't cope with embarrassment – he just doesn't know how to handle it. He'll walk away from any heated situation rather than stare it straight in the face. This was one such situation and true to form Rod turned and walked away with Britt on his arm, completely snubbing his former lover. It was as simple as that ... and Dee Harrington was on her way out.

From that moment on, Britt Ekland was number one, top of the popsies.

At first the singer and his new girl were ideally matched. Rod fell in love with Britt; in turn the actress was devoted to him. "I was more in love with Rod Stewart than with any other man past or present," she said in her memoirs. "When I give myself to a man, I am utterly at his command. Whatever he desires, I will do ... I have always been discriminating in the choice of lovers, but once in bed I'm like a slave.

"Our love-making was passionate – we couldn't keep our hands off each other for long. Rod regarded every orgasm as a testimony of our love.

Britt also admitted that she and her beau played sexual games trying to set up new records of endurance, improving on the standards set from the day before's work-out.

During all this time of "frenetic love-making" (Britt's words), Rod was still up to his old tricks. He simply couldn't keep his hands off other girls, and could never resist the chance of a bit on the side particularly as Britt was spending more and more time away from the un-marital home, either visiting her family in Scandinavia or trying to re-thread the needle of her former acting career.

So it wasn't long before that old favorite Bebe Buell came flying back into favor. Actress Susan George, too, who had met Rod and Britt at a Beverley Hills party some months before, spent many days – and nights – at the Stewart household while La Ekland was elsewhere detained.

Britt didn't care for Susan George at all and had taken an instant disliking to her. When they first met, Rod seemed fascinated with the English actress and spent much of the evening deep in conversation with her. *That* was too much for even Britt to accept. She was being totally ignored by her lover who in turn was captivated by *another woman*. She made a scene, slapped Mr. Stewart across the face, and flounced out of the party, leaving Susan in Rod's arms. A few months later, she was in his bed.

Liz Treadwell, the celebrated American model, was another willing partner in the bed-hopping stakes. Rod actually stole *her* affections away from actor George Hamilton – who was to lose his *wife* to Stewart later on – and on yet another occasion when Britt was on her travels, Liz actually moved into *their* home for the duration of the time Miss Ekland was out of town. She only moved out again a few hours before the Swedish actress arrived home. Incredibly, Britt suspected nothing of the affair – Rod must have made the bed. The neighbors too didn't let on, they'd had a field day with all the comings and goings.

Shortly afterwards, however, George Hamilton got his own back on Rod Stewart, and told Britt about the Liz Treadwell affair. When the singer later openly admitted spending the night with the American model, Britt was on *her* way out of the house ... and into the law courts. Not to mention the gossip columns.

It was amazing to everyone that the affair had lasted so long, especially after the Susan George incident. Very few people humiliated Rod in public and got away with it. Britt had ... but only just.

When Rod met the woman who was to become Mrs. Stewart – Alana Hamilton the former wife of actor George – his close friends again said it wouldn't last. But they had bargained *without* the very resourceful Ms. Hamilton. When they married, friends and foes alike were stunned!

Yet, Alana was different from all the other girls in Rod's life, even though she did have the basic requirements to become a Stewart floosey – long blonde hair, super boobs and long legs.

She came from a clean living, clean loving town in Texas – "where young girls never smoked or drank. They might kiss a boy ... but that was all they did. It never went further."

She was very independent and like Rod, Alana had always got her own way in any relationship. She was *always* the one to end any affair ... no-one ever walked out on her! But then, no-one had ever walked out on Rod. So really, they were ideally matched.

They met at a star-spangled party Rod threw in Los Angeles and the superstar was totally taken with this new girl in his life. So much so, that he took her to dinner the next evening. In a handful of days ... they were in love.

However, Alana decided *against* moving in with Super-Rod, despite his daily requests. She lived in her own house in the city and refused to live with him. And despite the fact that they both wanted children (Rod had certainly changed), to make their relationship complete, Alana refused point blank to become pregnant until plans had been made for marriage. Ms. Hamilton was certainly independent, certainly different, and Rod loved her for it. He did the decent thing, too, and proposed. They were married in April 1978. And their daughter Kimberley arrived in August 1979.

Not long after the birth, Rod told a British newspaper that "I've finally found someone who is everything I want, and when I'm with her I don't need other people. With every other girl it has been different." Was this really superstud Stewart talking?

"I love a girl with spunk who can stand up for herself and that's Alana." It certainly was.

"Bebe and Marcy were clinging wallflower-types. Britt was hardly that type, and that's why she lasted so long. But Alana's independence is what I like."

People in the know actually reported a great change in the superstar and when he became a father for the first time, the metamorphis was complete. He had certainly mellowed: "I don't feel tied down by my marriage," he added. And on being a father, he continued — "It's wonderful — I've no desire to mess about."

Alana echoed her husband's sentiments. "I'm not saying he's (Rod) turned into some boring old man with carpet slippers, but the fact is Rod doesn't feel the urge to live it up as much as he used to.

"I just hate people who assume that Rod Stewart is nothing more than an insolent womanizer. All right ... so he went out with a lot of women, but he was a good looking man — and all men like to sow their wild oats.

"But Rod believes in the sanctity of marriage as much as I do. I basically think if a man is happy at home and in love with the person he is with, I don't think he wants to go and pop into bed with any little groupie who comes along.

"The fact is, he wasn't ready to settle down until he met me. He waited till he picked the right person. I don't believe Rod ever intended to marry Britt Ekland. Never!"

There was certainly no love lost between the two ladies, and their open hatred for each other manifested itself on New Year's Eve in 1978.

Rod and his new wife attended a party in a London nightclub which was packed to the rafters with international celebrities. One such "star" was Britt Ekland who just happened to be celebrating the birth of the new year. When she spotted her old flame, she slunk across the dance floor, over to the table where he sat with a very attentive Alana, drinking champagne. In a great theatrical display, Miss Ekland threw her arms around Rod's neck and planted a passionate kiss on his lips. "Happy New Year, darling," she cried for everyone to hear.

Alana kept her cool. And promptly poured a glass of ice-cold champagne over Britt's head! The girl had style ... and Rod always liked a girl with style.

7
OMAR SHARIF
...A Wolf in Sheik's clothing

Omar Sharif quite simply is every woman's idea of *the* perfect Eastern lover. The man, they dream will one day ride out of the sun on a white charger and carry them off to his tent in the desert for a wild night of passion and frenzy. And no wonder ...

He is tall – nearing six foot – dark and craggily good-looking. His rich, dark brown voice – with just a trace of accent – has captivated millions of women movie lovers, while his dark brown penetrating eyes have melted the iciest heart. Many of the women who have known him – and there have been quite a few – have admitted to being "undressed" and "seduced" by his eyes alone. Even actress Sophia Loren told of being caressed by them.

Omar owes a lot to that particular part of his anatomy. (He also owes a lot to another part, but that's another story.) It was his dark and mysterious eyes that virtually clinches his appearance in the block-busting picture "Lawrence Of Arabia", the film that brought him to the attention of the world.

When director David Lean was casting the movie, he needed an Arab actor to play the part of Sherif-Ali. Not just any common or desert Arab would do, he *had* to be true to life and have dark eyes and dark features to contrast against the blond features and blue eyes of Peter O'Toole, who was playing Lawrence. He looked all over the world without success.

A month before shooting started, French actor Maurice Ronet *was* signed for the part by Sam Spiegel. True enough, he had dark, almost Arabian features, but when David Lean found out he had *GREEN* eyes, he was furious!

"He won't do!" he told his assistants. "Get me photos of every Arab actor. There's got to be one who's just right!"

Omar Sharif was just right. He got the part.

"Lawrence of Arabia" was the film that launched Omar Sharif not only as an international actor, but as an international playboy and the great Eastern lover! He was ideal fodder for the gossip columnists, too, the last of the matinee idols in the mold of Valentino and Novarro. And when it was revealed that he was a gambler and womanizer as well, who liked to live hard, to play hard … and love a little roughly, too, the Press really went to town. They actually helped to foster his reputation as a lady-killer and superstud. As one newspaper later put it, Omar "was a kind of Aswan Dam of sex, he exuded an enthralling aura of wild stallions". It was a compliment and Omar didn't mind, he was having a good time and didn't want to let the readers down. So he played his part of the wolf in Sheik's clothing, preying on every woman who came along and fell for the hypnotic eyes, that were full of Eastern promise!

When he first arrived in Hollywood to promote "Lawrence", Omar was regularly seen in the company of beautiful women at all the right high society parties and balls, where he admitted to flirting with the girls. It certainly didn't end there. He escorted glamorous up-and-coming starlets to other beanfeasts arranged by the top show business P.R. men. Needless to say, the Press were tipped off whenever he made a move, and dutifully reported the events in the morning newspapers. His reputation was growing. "He had more beautiful women thrown at him than Alhabama has had hot gospel singers," was the phrase one newspaper later used to describe his success with women.

In his memoirs, though, Omar refused to talk about his affairs in those early days in Hollywood. He said: "I neither want to mention them nor have I the right to do so. Gallantry forbids from doing this … I don't think any man can devise glory and benefit from being the husband or lover of Omar Sharif's mistress."

He has always remained the perfect gentleman, however, which is hardly the image a rampant superstud conjures up. Still, maybe the Press got it wrong again. Actress Alexandra Bastedo certainly believes so. They had a brief encounter in the mid-1970's. "He is a super person," she said. "He is a very sensitive and kind person and not at all like his playboy image."

Omar agreed. "I'm not really a playboy at all. It's just that I am *available* as a man which is the common denominator of playboys, I think. Hostesses adore the spare man.

"I have a very normal sex-life — even substandard. Most men do as well if not better. The only difference is they don't read about it in the newspapers afterwards.

"My reputation as a heart-throb puts girls off — I have to fight for my girlfriends. It's really a drawback having the kind of reputation I have. The girl is expecting some kind of miracle performance."

Yet despite what he *might* say, Omar most certainly is able to give good value for as yet, no-one has complained. And he still seems to be able to collect women like most other men collect stamps. Indeed he has been seen with Catherine Deneuve, Ava Gardner, Barbra Streisand, Barbara Bouchet, Claudia Cardinale, Dyan Cannon, Imogen Hassall … and a few more besides. It is a veritable Arabian harem.

"I worship women!" he says. "I get any woman I want because I give of myself. And who can refuse such human warmth? If all my affairs have been satisfactory it's because of my total understanding of women. I can satisfy all of their desires.

"Egyptian men really are very good in bed — I think it's because from boyhood it's the only thing on their minds!"

He told one journalist: "You know a man likes to go to bed with lots of girls, but he doesn't like to wake up with all of them in the morning.

"I often wake up and look at the girl beside me and think – oh, I wish she wasn't here.

"If I really like a girl, after a time I ask her to come and stay with me in Paris." He owns a luxury bachelor apartment, overlooking the Bois de Boulogne, which he designed himself. All the bedrooms are downstairs with the games rooms upstairs, and marble baths the size of most bedrooms.

"I'll take a girl out a few times – and if we hit it off, I'll invite her to move in with me. After a week, I'll know if I've made a mistake. If it's not right any more, then we go our separate ways. But, to be frank, my interest in any particular woman lasts a few days, then boredom sets in."

He admitted to another: "I'm an incurable romantic. That's what life is all about. All the time I'm looking for the right girl. I haven't found her yet, but I'm not going to stop trying.

Omar Sharif does have his own set ideas on the kind of girl he is looking for, and he has certainly tried out a few of them to enable him to draw up his perfect blueprint.

"My kind of woman can be of any size, any color, as long as she's nice. But if she doesn't know how to cook, she won't be feminine enough for me.

"A woman has to be interested in my body. There are ways of touching that are important to me. Being good in bed is a gift. A woman should work at being good. It's *her* pleasure in doing it that makes her good – not her doing it to give *you* pleasure.

"Making love? Is like communion with a woman – the bed is the holy table. There I find passion and purification. For me one love drives away another – and the woman who is inspiring the love at that time fills my entire world."

He should certainly know what he's talking about, he has made a study of the subject, and during his time as an international playboy, he has made love to women from all over the world. He told a Sunday newspaper: "Dutch girls are the best in the world. They keep going all night. Australian girls are so good, very athletic. Hungarians are rather special too. Scandinavian girls aren't all they are cracked up to be. They've absolutely no inhibitions about sex, but it's over too quickly. Germans are enthusiastic, but too mechanical. You probably see more pretty girls in England than anywhere else, but they have no style, no finesse, no sophistication.

"French women are totally feminine, totally dedicated to pleasing their man and working hard at making the most of themselves. If I do ever re-marry, it will be to a French girl.

"Americans are the worst in the world. I have come to dislike them intensely."

Omar Sharif was born Michael Shalhoub on April 10th, 1932, in Alexandria, Egypt, of Lebanese-Syrian stock. He was christened into the Roman Catholic faith.

His father was a wealthy timber merchant, who spoiled his son. His mother liked to play cards and gambled, sometimes beyond her means. She belonged to a close knit circle whose numbers included King Farouk himself, and he became a regular visitor to the Shalhoub house in Cairo to where the family had moved when their young son was four years old.

Michael Shalhoub was sent to the best schools money could buy and was given a

French education until he was ten. Then he was sent to an English Secondary school in Cairo.

He was a plump and very awkward little boy, but he excelled at his studies particularly maths, and also developed a great love for soccer, becoming skilled at the game once he had slimmed down considerably. Another great interest in his life at that time, was drama and he spent many hours at the school theater group where he enjoyed entertaining his fellow students.

On his sixteenth birthday his father gave him a car as a present and told him to go out and enjoy himself.

"My father encouraged me to indulge as much as I liked in drink and women," said Omar. But he drew the line at his acting — which he thought was a passing phase his son would soon tire of — and gambling. "His theory was that man can be totally ruined by gambling, but can hardly lose his fortune through drink and women, only some of it!"

And it was at about the same time, that Omar had his first sexual encounter, albeit with a local prostitute in the back of his parked car in a make-shift desert car park, not far from the airport. It was the Egyptian equivalent of Lovers Lane. Still, the experience gave him a great liking for sex — "they've never found a substitute for it" — and a passion for prostitutes — "I love whores, too." During the breaks in the filming of "Lawrence Of Arabia", which were limited to two or three days at the end of each month's work, he and Peter O'Toole went hunting girls together in the bars and nightclubs of Beirut.

When Michael left school, he joined his father's timber business and ran a small amateur theater group in his spare time. At the age of twenty, however, he decided to take up acting full-time, when he was asked to appear in a domestic movie called "The Blazing Sun" by one of his old friends, Jusef Shadine, who was directing the film. It proved to be one of the most important movies he ever made — for it was during shooting that Michael Shalhoub disappeared, to be replaced by Omar Sharif.

The story goes that he chose the name OMAR because it sounded very Middle Eastern, which was his first consideration, and it was easily spelt in almost any language; though another suggests that he named himself after the American General Omar Bradley. For the surname, however, Omar wanted to be called SHERIF — an Arabian word for noble birth, but he thought it sounded too much like the English word sheriff. So he adapted it slightly to SHARIF. But that's his story. While he was making "Lawrence of Arabia", Peter O'Toole would have none of it, and nicknamed him "Cairo Fred".

On the set of that first film "The Blazing Sun", newly named Sharif met his future wife, actress Faten Hamama — who at that time was the country's most celebrated and most famous film star. Omar caused a huge outcry throughout Egypt shortly after their meeting, when he became the first person *ever* to kiss the actress on the screen! He was the subject of tremendous scorn and scandal in the Egyptian Press. Needless to say, the publicity the kiss attracted made the film a sure-fire box-office success.

Away from the screen, Omar's attention to the actress's details didn't stop at kissing. They became lovers ... and eventually decided to marry, even though Faten already had a husband and young daughter. But the marriage problem was soon overcome and they married in February 1955, after Omar had first renounced his

Catholic faith in favor of becoming a Mohammedan. Their son Tarek was born two years later.

For the next few years, Omar Sharif made many films in Egypt including half-a-dozen or so with his wife, which were all guaranteed box-office successes. He soon established himself as one of his country's finest actors. In 1960, David Lean changed all that and two years later, with the release of "Lawrence Of Arabia", he was a world star and hailed as one of the most desirable men in the world! At one time, he received no less than 25,000 marriage proposals each month! His own marriage lasted until 1966. "By then domestic life had lost its attraction," he said, and his wife "had stopped being exciting". They went their separate ways.

Since emerging, according to one newspaper as "the heart throb screen lover who exists for women alone", Cairo Fred's name has been linked with almost every available actress or girl-about-town within kissing distance and certainly with all of his leading ladies, including Barbra Streisand.

They met when they made "Funny Girl" together in 1968, and had an affair.

"I fell madly in love with her talent and her personality," he said. "The feeling was mutual for four months — the time it took for shooting the picture. How many of my affairs seemed to last till the end of shooting?"

They spent most of their spare time together, evenings and weekends at her villa where "we led the very simple life of people in love". For once news of the affair *didn't* reach the newspapers until it was all over.

However, the two superstars were involved in a slight political scandal while making the movie resulting from the fact that Barbra was Jewish; Omar was an Arab!

"One Egyptian magazine published a picture of me kissing Streisand," he said.

"And it said — 'Bar this actor from Arab nationality'. But my answer was that I never ask a girl her religion before kissing her."

It was the second time in his career that a simple screen kiss had caused him to be pilloried by the Press in his native country!

He met French actress Anouk Aimée when they made "The Appointment" together. They too, had an affair and Omar called her "the world's most extraordinary woman" and even considered marriage. "She was without the slightest doubt a fine girl who had qualities that I'd never suspected in a woman. Anouk knows how to act with the man she loves. She knows how to please him, she knows all the things her man likes and wants, and at the precise moment he likes them or wants them.

"Anouk was the ideal companion. There was a time when I thought we could make our lives together."

They never did marry — "the need to safeguard my independence must have won out" — and that is one of the reasons he believes he will never marry again.

"How can I have a regular girl friend? I've got all these impossible bachelor habits. I like to lie in bed reading sometimes till six in the morning. It's my favorite moment of the day. What girl would stand for it? And I'm lazy ... I like to find my toothbrush where I left it."

When beautiful Egyptian actress Suheir Ramzi announced to the world in 1977 that she had just become the second Mrs. Sharif — Omar was furious! "She's amazing — I don't plan to get married. If I did, it would have to be to a woman who really swept me off my feet. If she is interested in bridge, so much the better. If she is interested in horses, so much the better — she's got to love all that — and also be intelligent and exciting in bed. I don't know if I'll ever find her, but it'll be miserable the day I stop trying and give up".

It's hard to believe, but according to Cairo Fred himself, women have always taken *third* place in the Sharif pecking order, behind his great love for horses and bridge. "They will take over as my interest in women declines!" Is this really Omar talking?

"When I was young it was all work and women, but when you become older, your hobbies become your passions.

"Bridge is even better than that other greater indoor sport, making love — because there you reach your peak and gradually decline. In bridge you never reach your peak." Omar doesn't do too badly at either — *but* he is a world champion bridge-player and has captained his country in major tournaments. He regularly tours the world with other champion players giving exhibition matches. Such is his fanaticism for the cards that at first he refused to make the movie "The Yellow Rolls Royce" because the shooting schedules clashed with a major tournament. The producer decided to alter the schedules ...

But he readily admits that his Number One passion of all, is for his magnificent horses which he stables in Normandy. He also owns a renowned stud farm in Ireland, near Dublin. "I would take any film, no matter how bad, to pay for my horses." That is how dedicated he is!

There can be no denying, that like most of the world's great superstud characters, Omar Sharif is a typical chauvinist! He certainly likes to do things *his* way when it comes to women. He likes to dominate them.

"I've no time for Women's Lib. What does all that mean ... that they want to go to bed with just anybody, or that they want to run General Motors? *I* want to be the one to give liberation to my women.

"Women who don't have a man to call the shots are terribly unhappy. What they want is a man to master them and dominate them.

"Look at American women, the most liberated in the world. They all make fools of themselves going off to Europe on holiday and longing to find an Italian male – some chic Valentine – who will sweep them off *their* feet. They *want* to be carried off into the desert and dumped in a tent. But then there isn't a woman alive who hasn't dreamt of one wild night of passion with an Eastern lover in the desert."

... And there are very few women who haven't dreamt of that Eastern lover being Omar Sharif!

8
RYAN O'NEAL
...*Always* the Main Event

If Ryan O'Neal is as good at making love, as he is at fighting, then it's easy to see why he has made his reputation as a modern-day Errol Flynn *and* the man one newspaper hailed as ''Hollywood's Number One Romeo''.

Quite simply, he must be dynamite in every sense of the word.

Yet, for the man with a liberal helping of Irish blood in his veins, Ryan also has a very short fuse, which is guaranteed to ignite with the minimum amount of provocation.

Since establishing himself as something of a force-to-be-reckoned-with in the superstar acting stakes through such films as ''Love Story'' and ''Paper Moon'', O'Neal has made nearly as many headlines for his exploits with his fists — notably through public brawling with newspaper reporters and photographers — than with another more delicate part of his anatomy. And in Ryan's case, with his track record, that takes some doing.

The O'Neal hell-raising started when he was a teenager and very much into chasing girls, drinking and drugs — a little later in life, he was put on probation after being found guilty of possession — and very little else.

''At University High School I knew life was a fun time. Part of the fun was getting into a lot of fights and trying to make the girls go all the way,'' he once said, and proved his point time and time again.

When he was eighteen, however, the fighting landed him in trouble when he was convicted of assault and battery after one particular night of pugilistic pyrotechnics and sent to prison. Two months behind locked doors, though, only served to heighten his passion for trading punches whenever the opportunity arose. Even when he emerged from almost total obscurity into the limelight of recognition as an actor, his high spirits couldn't be halted. Some of the Hollywood gossip mongers often hinted

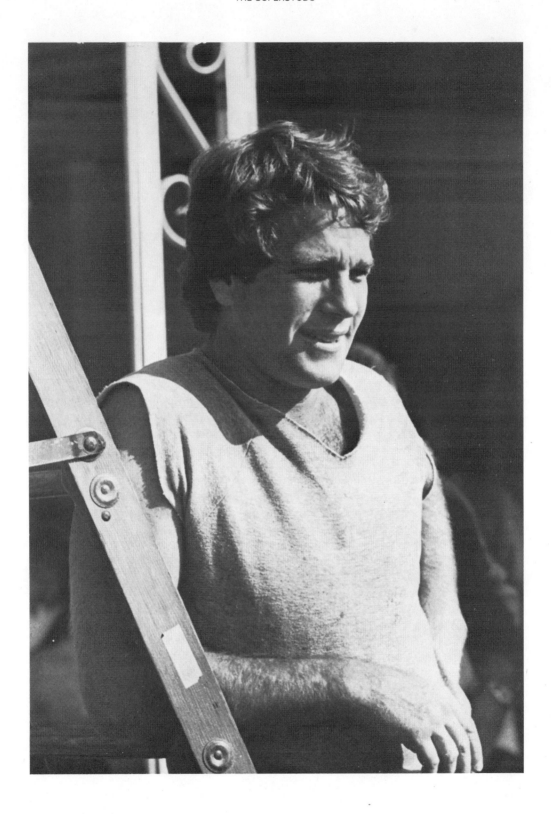

that he went out looking for trouble intentionally, as a way of keeping the publicity fires burning and his name in the papers. Like Flynn, any publicity was good publicity so long as they spelled the name correctly. He was after notoriety and it didn't take him too long to find it!

Romeo Ryan's public exploits of fisticuffs have become well documented in the Press. He once set about an English journalist, in the lobby of a Five Star London Hotel simply because he didn't much care for the line of questioning the interviewer was taking. He also attacked his former publicity agent, Steve Jaffe, in the middle of a swank Hollywood party and sent him flying across a table. He hit Jaffe's wife, actress Susan Blakely, too, who later floored the superstar by bringing a million dollar lawsuit against him for assault.

He knocked a New Orleans journalist cold for "being too aggressive" with his then girl of the moment Barbara Parkins. "It was a perfect punch," Ryan admitted later with great pride. And he pinned a Fleet Street photographer against a wall at Heathrow Airport after the cameraman got "far too close" to his *then* girl of the moment Farrah Fawcett. "Don't you ever touch her," he yelled and then proceeded to choke the Englishman.

Even former wife Joanna Moore — they married in 1963 — admitted: "Ryan and I used to have knock-down fights, but he wouldn't hesitate to hit a guy who said something to offend me. He's *all man*!"

Actually the first Mrs. O'Neal couldn't have said a truer word, for her husband has worked very hard over the years at cultivating his image as the all-American tough guy who nearly always ends up with the girl.

Joanna added: "Women tend to want to go to bed with him." And Ryan tends to want to go to bed with them, too! "I have an insatiable appetite for girls," he has said on many occasions. And over the years that appetite has voraciously "eaten up" the like of Barbra Streisand — with whom he made two movies "What's Up Doc" and "The Main Event" — ("I did love Barbra"); singer-songwriters Carole King — who wrote a song about him — and Joni Mitchell, who called him "warm and sensitive"; Ali MacGraw, who said he made her "feel like a woman"; Marisa Barenson; French actress Anouk Aimée; Beverley Adams; and Lana Wood.

He had a brief liaison with Bianca Jagger ("Terrific girl") après Mick; paid court to Liza Minelli; and, in August 1979, admitted to "falling in love with Oona" (Chaplin) — widow of Charlie Chaplin — who was fourteen years his senior.

Joan Collins rated his performance under the bed clothes as *"five"*. She didn't, however, clarify her marking system — though perhaps she was using the Richter Scale, for measuring earthquakes! And Ryan's score *could* have been for how much the earth moved when they made love together. He actually made love to her for the very first time, on her birthday — though she declined to say which one she was celebrating at the time — when her then husband Tony Newley was out of town.

"Ryan had it all going for him in the looks department", she said. "And he wasn't lacking in the charm and humor departments either ... or the sex appeal department.

"Ryan was a terrific, imaginative and inventive lover. In fact, inventiveness was one of his strong points."

Britt Ekland echoed: "Our sleeping together became more and more under the heading of comfort and consolation between two old friends."

And Mynah Bird revealed his secret fetish. "He took off my shoe, grabbed hold of my naked foot and started kissing it – he called it . . . the sexiest part of my body." Ah, well, there's no accounting for taste!

Yet despite the women flooding to his front door, Ryan O'Neal is very single-minded in his approach to females. "Quite frankly, I am incapable of being faithful," he has said. "I don't find it easy to fall in love. Deep love is not an easy act for me, so much else goes with it. Selflessness for instance and I haven't got that!" Still he does know exactly what he wants and stops at nothing until he gets it. If that means hurting a few people along the way. So be it.

He once relieved actor Jack Nicholson of his girl friend Anjelica Huston, leaving Jack to go bleating to the newspapers. "Ryan O'Neal *was* a friend of mine. Now I'm not happy to be seen in the same town or mentioned in the same sentence with him."

Jon Peters, live-in boyfriend of Barbra Streisand, had heard all about O'Neal's reputation as a woman-taker, and he was very aware that Ryan and Streisand had had a passionate and much-publicized affair in the early 1970's. So, when it came to their making "The Main Event" together, he was very apprehensive about them sharing the movie's love scenes. "It's pretty hard to watch your old lady making it with someone else," he said. "Specially her former lover." He needn't have worried, Ryan's affections were elsewhere at that time.

But his most famous lady snatching act came when he actually coaxed Farrah Fawcett away from her husband Lee Majors, right in front of the Six Million Dollar Man's eyes.

The love-match came about in September 1979 when Ryan asked his old buddy Lee Majors for an introduction to Cheryl Ladd on the set of "Charlie's Angels", where Farrah just happened to be filming a guest-appearance in the popular television show. But as soon as O'Neal saw the voluptuous Mrs. Fawcett-Majors, he was totally captivated by her, and completely forgot his interest in Ms. Ladd. The feeling, as far as Farrah was concerned, was mutual. "I guess he did sweep me off my feet," she said, eyes glinting.

After that first meeting, Lee Majors made the fatal mistake of asking Ryan to keep an eye on his wife during their much publicized trial separation. O'Neal was only too pleased to help his friend out.

"He certainly kept *more* than an eye on her," said a shattered Lee Majors, shortly afterwards.

Patrick Ryan O'Neal was born into an Irish-American family in Hollywood, California in April 1941. His father Charlie O'Neal was a film and television script-writer, and his mother, Patricia, a former actress. So the chances were the the young Ryan would eventually end up in the business in some department or other. And he saw a lot of showbusiness in the early days, as the family travelled the world with Charlie, who was regularly jetting off for location work.

When Ryan was eighteen – just after his stint in prison – he accompanied his father to Munich, Germany, where he was writing scripts on location for an American television serial. Charlie wanted to curb his rebel-rousing son's high spirits once and for all and made arrangements for him to complete his education at the US Army High School in the German city. But Ryan, had other ideas, and in almost open defiance of his father's wishes, he took a job as an extra on the same TV series. He increased his money when he doubled as a stunt man.

Back home in Los Angeles, he prepared to unleash his brilliant (his word) acting ability on to an unsuspecting public. The trouble was no-one had as much faith in his talent as *he* did. Parts were hard to come by, particularly for a newcomer with limited experience. So Ryan was forced to try his hand at other things until the right opportunities presented themselves. He took any job that came along and worked as a life-guard, truck driver, odd-job man, waiter and even washed dishes in a local restaurant.

However, the big break was on the horizon. He was signed up to play opposite Charles Bronson in the cowboy TV series, "Empire", which was later to lead to his playing the college-boy playboy Rodney Harrington in television's continuing story of "Peyton Place". And *that* was perfect type-casting.

In 1963, sometime before he started shooting the TV soap opera, Ryan O'Neal met a beautiful actress named Joanna Moore, during the filming of "Empire". She was thirty-one, nine years older than him, yet they hit it off immediately, and were soon constant companions ... in and out of the bedroom.

"Joanna was pregnant within a few days of our meeting," said Ryan with pride. They virtually *had* to get married and the wedding took place on April 3rd, 1963. He was ever true to his word, too, for seven months after the ceremony, daughter Tatum was born. Yet the marriage was in trouble right from the beginning. Ryan was out of work more often than not, and was left at home to mind the baby while his wife went out and earned a very good living, appearing in television films.

"I was Tatum's nanny. Her mother was working ... I trained her, fed her, cared for her," said Ryan.

Naturally, he resented the fact that his wife was regularly employed while *he* couldn't even find a job. Any job. The couple started fighting in private *and* in public. It was inevitable that the relationship was heading for the scrap yard and even the arrival of son Griffin altered nothing.

The final death knell for the marriage tolled when Ryan landed the part in "Peyton Place". His confidence returned, and with it, his roving eye for the girls. It didn't take too long before the gossip columnists were linking his name romantically with his leading ladies and several of the young actresses who made guest appearances in the long running show. It wasn't idle gossip, either. Most of the time, Ryan was playing around with whoever would be his partner.

One of his favorite tricks in the early days of his budding career, was to take his latest flame to a nearby studio bar for a drink. He had already made arrangements with the waitresses there, to serve the girls doubles, while he was given something less potent. Ryan hadn't quite worked out the line in charm then and had to rely on getting his women drunk before he even attempted seduction. Still, they were early days. He was learning all the time.

His marriage to Joanna Moore drifted on for a further few months, and then both parties decided to call it a day. Tatum was two years old, her brother Griffin, one – and naturally they stayed with their mother. Ryan didn't mind, he was living life to the full again with any girl who wanted to get involved. There were plenty of takers, too.

He met his second wife Leigh Taylor-Young, during the filming of "Peyton Place". The doe-eyed young actress joined the show as a replacement for Mia Farrow, who

had left in a blaze of publicity some months before. Again, O'Neal was totally enthralled by the young starlet. He described her as being "sensual and womanly", and added – "Leigh is beautiful – a lovely woman. There's a peacefulness about her, a tranquility; I have always needed that influence."

The inevitable love affair followed, and Leigh, like her predecessor, became pregnant almost immediately. Then the problems really started!

Ryan was *still* married to Joanna Moore and had to go, cap is hand, to beg her for a divorce. But his luck was in and she agreed. On the same day as the decree was granted, he and Leigh were married and the Press likened it to a marriage between "Tarzan and Mary Poppins". It was doomed to failure.

After their son Patrick was born, they worked together on the movie "The Big Bounce" and then Ryan's career almost came to an abrupt full stop, while his wife's started to pick up.

"What are you supposed to feel when your beautiful wife goes to work?" he said. "Bitter and frustrated!" His suspect temper couldn't be calmed, and he fought with Leigh almost nonstop. "You'll never see us fighting in the streets – but don't come home." Ryan was almost proud of the situation!

There was another problem, too. "Leigh didn't like me playing around with other women," he said. "That's why we broke up. I *had* to stay married ... I *had* to be faithful ... but I just couldn't manage it."

Rumors were circulating around Hollywood that this second marriage was going the same way as the first. Ryan did his best, however, to dispel them. When American TV personality Rona Barrett announced to her viewers that the O'Neal marriage was in ruins and that Ryan and Leigh had split up, he retaliated by sending her a *live* tarrantula spider as a present!

But soon, no amount of denials could plaster over the cracks. Four years after the wedding ceremony, the marriage finally ended. Ryan had inevitably met someone else – this time it was Barbra Streisand – and Leigh had simply had enough. *He* was twenty-nine.

"When I was growing up," he said, "I had two rules. One was not to get married. The other was not to have children. I blew it. Twice."

After the divorce, Ryan O'Neal went on a great charge of drinking and womanizing. It was as if he was out to prove something to himself and the world.

"I know I won a reputation as a famous heartbreaker by being something of a wild boy," he told one newspaper, and then spent every moment he could trying to live up to it. "When I'm depressed or disappointed, I drink or run after girls – or both. I guess I'm not very likable. But I don't care too much."

One woman did, however, manage to tame the rebel. His young daughter Tatum. He told a newspaper: "One day, this funny little girl of eight, with an old man's voice, arrived on my doorstep carrying her suitcase. Tatum said – 'I would like to stay'. I said I had no nanny and that I moved very fast! She said that would be okay. She wouldn't get in the way.

"Of course, she *was* in the way, but it didn't matter. Tatum was so fabulous. Despite all those stories of me and girls, I was really lonely.

"I may have difficulty committing myself to one woman, but I had no trouble at all committing myself to Tatum".

... And Tatum has been a standard furnishing and fixture in the O'Neal house ever since. Ryan was granted custody from Joanna Moore a few months after his daughter tapped on his door. They even starred together in one of Ryan's most famous, and most successful movies, "Paper Moon", when Tatum was just nine years old.

O'Neal had actually found his first wife "living in a shack with a dying horse and a dead chicken and growing flowers in a wrecked car", he told reporters at the time. She was very heavily involved with drugs.

Tatum O'Neal has a permanent place in Ryan's life. "She has a good effect on me," he says. "She's seen all my warts" – She even vets the women in his life, though, *he* says she doesn't mind him bringing girls home because they can help with the cooking.

The young Miss O'Neal, however, has shown open hostility to some of his more famous conquests and disapproved violently of his affair with Margaret Trudeau. "She left scratch marks on our gate post – that's all I'll say," she admitted, afterwards. Tatum was also reported spitting at another one she didn't like.

However, she did approve of Diana Ross who, said Ryan, was her choice as the next Mrs. O'Neal. Their affair didn't last long enough for that.

Tatum also gave the thumbs up to Ursula Andress, who lived with the O'Neals at their home in Malibu and spent many weeks body surfing naked with Ryan in the Pacific Ocean.

"Tatum adored her. When Ursula Andress was here, she was forever putting on her bracelets and being scolded by her. Females are wonderful, they need each other."

She gave the nod of approval to Farrah Fawcett, too. "She's sensible," said Tatum. "And that's just what my father needs ... a sensible woman". Though she did draw the line at her father marrying for the third time.

"I don't want him to marry again – ever. Why should he commit himself again? We have a nice thing going at home, so why bring anyone else in?"

It's a sentiment echoed by dad: "I'm not re-marrying! Certainly not for the sake of giving Tatum another mother. Marriage is hard enough without *that!* Tatum watches over me so. She'll never accept another woman."

As he grows older, Ryan O'Neal has quietened down considerably. He is still very much a Jekyll and Hyde personality, though. One minute he is charm itself, the perfect gentleman and host. The next, the old fuse box blows again and he becomes mean and moody, and violent ... ready to do his talking with his fists.

But he *is* trying to live down the glamor boy image, the playboy who is always on the look out for girls, and he hopes to re-write some of the nastier things said about him in the past. He wants to put the record straight – *his* way.

"I know I'm always being portrayed as a playboy, but it's ridiculous. How can I be a playboy with Tatum sleeping on my bed? Where is all the excitement taking place?

"Listen I understand that people may be interested in what I do. But it doesn't mean I have to *like it. Or* talk about it."

... Which is strange because for the past fifteen years, Ryan O'Neal has done nothing, but talk about it!

9
TOM JONES
...The Welsh have a word for it too!

Tom Jones doesn't mind who knows it: he adores his reputation as a superstud and everything it stands for.

He works hard, too, at preserving the image, and keeping journalists well fuelled with sexy pictures and stories. He told one – "My sex image symbol is all fun really. Women still throw their panties at me on stage, thank God.

"As long as they see me that way, that's the way I'll be. I like being a sex symbol, but my wife doesn't think much of it. She doesn't really like it.

It is an act – and it's brilliant!

On stage, he oozes earthy sex appeal from every part of his well tanned and healthy body that is literally poured into a tight-fitting, black evening suit. The trousers are so tight – they are hand-tailored to fit the actual curves of his legs – that it is as easy, to make out his religion as it is to recognize his gender, if that was ever in doubt.

Still, it's enough to drive even the most conservative fan wild. The Jones' act is pure, unadulterated sex. Nothing more. "I know what women want," says Tom. "And I give it to them. When I go out on stage, I just concentrate on being as sexy as I can!"

He belts out each song in his distinctive blues-cum-soul voice, gyrating and thrusting his well-kept body to the pulsating beat of the music that reverberates all around him. It's animal magnetism at its most basic. Erotic! Sizzling! Sensuous! And the audience love every single minute. Grown women – not just teenyboppers – who are driven wild, rip off their bras and panties (sometimes both) and hurl them to the stage, at the feet of their superhero. Others call out the most lurid sexual suggestions of which most are impossible!

Tom Jones – hailed by one English newspaper as "one of the world's most potent sex symbols" certainly does possess an amazing power over women. And there are

many hundreds of them who would dearly love him to exercise that power over them ...

"When I see the women coming down to the stage," he says. "Then I know I'm getting to them ... and that's a good feeling. I like to have fun on stage, but I always make fun of myself. That's the secret."

Tom likes to have a little fun off stage, too, and over the years, rumors have been rife about his close encounters of the sexual kind with some of the world's most adorable ladies. Yet, Jones The Voice is quick to defend himself. "I wouldn't be human if I said that I didn't fancy other women and I don't suppose I'm different to any other married man. But that's as far as it goes."

Still, his name *has* been mentioned in the same sentence with many women in the past, including every-man's-favorite-sex-symbol Raquel Welch and former Miss World, Marjorie Wallace.

There was nothing in the Raquel story, though, although some say she was very keen. Tom told close friends that he couldn't stand her, and then called her some rather unsavory names.

The Marjorie Wallace affair cut a little deeper. It made headlines all over the world especially after one newspaper discovered that Miss Wallace had kept a diary of her sexual activities, in which she rated her lovers' performances in bed out of a maximum score of ten! Tom Jones, they said, scored nine out of ten, while another of her famous sleeping companions, footballer George Best, could only manage three!

Tom first met Marjorie Wallace late in 1973 when they were both in London – she was an entrant for the Miss World competition; he was starring in concert at the London Palladium. But the tongues really started wagging at the beginning of the next year when Marjorie, now crowned as "the most beautiful girl in the world", joined Tom to appear in his BBC Television "special" – "Tom Jones On Happiness Island" – which was being filmed in Barbados. The Press hastily followed.

And during the few days they spent together on the island, Tom and Marji were inseparable. They went everywhere together hand-in-hand and they were anything but discreet. They were seen kissing in public and pictured gazing, longingly into each other's eyes as if they were passionate lovers. For all the newspapers knew, of course, they were.

The Press went to town again not long afterwards when the show was screened on TV, for in one scene Tom and Marji embraced and kissed with such intensity that it was obviously the result of a much more lasting relationship. It all started to make sense.

The story was hot news for a long time to come and it reached a peak just a few weeks later when Marjorie Wallace was relieved of her Miss World crown and unceremoniously dropped by the organizers of the competition because of the harmful publicity her affairs with Tom Jones and George Best had caused.

Losing the title didn't make a scrap of difference. Marji was still very much in the news and her on-and-off relationship with the Welsh singing star was very much the stuff of which newspapers were sold. And many thousands more were sold later in the year, when Tom Jones opened for a cabaret season in Las Vegas, particularly as Miss Wallace was found to be at his side on every night of his lengthy engagement. Still, she did have an alibi for being in Vegas. She was staying with her mother who just happened to live in the Nevada gambling town. But it didn't satisfy the Press ... they were after a much bigger story. When one intrepid photographer later snapped a picture of Marji sunning herself by Tom's swimming pool, her alibi was torn to shreds.

That incident helped to hurry the relationship to a close, though it almost ended in tragedy a few days later when Marjorie was rushed to hospital in her home town of Indianapolis after taking a massive overdose of sleeping pills. It was touch and go whether she survived. Only great vigilance on behalf of the hospital staff pulled her through. However, the affair with Tom Jones had ended.

Despite his position as one of the world's leading entertainers — able to pick and choose his women from almost any that might take his fancy — Tom Jones has had few affairs with the world's most celebrated females. He tends to shy away from them. It's much safer. In the past, according to one scandal sheet's great revelations in 1977, he has played it all very close to his hairy chest preferring to dally only with the female fans who not only throw their underwear at his feet, when he's on stage, but throw their entire bodies in his direction after the curtain has come down.

"When you're in the process of making love" said Tom, "the woman seems everything to you. After you have made love, she is one of two things; someone you want to keep with you — or someone you want to crawl away from." And if we are to believe the newspapers, when it came to women, Tom chose the latter. After all, he was supposed to be a superstud. But he did have his own ground rules — and one was that he never had anything to do with married women. They were strictly out of bounds, and had husbands to go back home to!

He did, however, become involved with two famous singers, both black and both beautiful — Nancy Wilson, and the former Supremes singing star Mary Wilson. He was also reported to have become entangled with model Joyce Ingalls.

Yet it was the affair with Mary Wilson which very nearly broke up his marriage in 1968. The liaison had been long established by the time Tom Jones was appearing in summer season in England in 1968, and the American singing star flew in to Britain to join him. She even set herself up in the house he was living in at the seaside resort, and was there for a long stay.

News of the affair filtered back to the press, and it was soon being hinted at in all the gossip columns. It didn't take long to reach the ears of Tom's lovely wife Linda. When one newspaper suggested that Mary Wilson had actually moved in to live with Tom, Linda decided to go and see for herself.

A series of frantic warning telephone calls from Tom's close friends followed, and the singing Supreme was whisked out of the house in record time, taking with her all her possessions. In fact every single trace of the woman was removed from the house, so that when Linda arrived, she found nothing that could have made her at all suspicious. But it was a close shave!

Tom Jones would be lost without his wife Linda — he admits it. It is to her that he owes his success. She was his first girl friend and his first love.

"She lived round the corner from me and we played together as kids," said Tom. "We grew up as sweethearts and all our friends knew we would marry eventually.

"If she was out somewhere and I wasn't with her, my pals wouldn't allow anyone else to bother her. She was my girl and everyone respected that."

They did marry — at sixteen — and within a year, their son Mark was born.

When he was unknown and living rough in London trying to find stardom, Linda stayed in Wales and looked after their son. "We were so poorly off, that Linda had to take a job in a factory to support herself and Mark. For her to have to go out to work because her husband couldn't support her, nearly brought me down — I never forgot those days and her loyalty."

Tom himself was born Thomas Woodward on June 7th, 1940, in Pontypridd, South Wales. And was named after his coal-miner father.

As a child, young Tom joined the chapel choir and was greatly influenced by traditional Welsh Hymns. He was however, expelled from the school choir after he was caught harmonizing on the national anthem. Away from school he sang for customers on an orange box platform in the local corner shop.

When he left Treforrest Secondary Modern School, he tried his hand at a number of jobs, including a building laborer for which he earned the grand sum of $40 a week ... and that to him was a small fortune.

"I became interested in showbusiness the moment I realized just how heavy a hod was," he said.

Tom had wanted to be a singer from the early days in the choir, and he worked hard at achieving that ambition.

"When I was a little boy," he admitted. "I always had this feeling that I was going to be a star. I told people I was going to be a famous singer, too. But I guess that all kids think that they are going to be something! Later on I realized it wasn't that easy, there were many other singers and I knew it was going to be a struggle."

Still, success came to Jones early in life, particularly with women.

"He was always a bit of a tearaway as far as women were concerned," said a former friend who helped him in the early stages of his career. "Tom was *always* on the look out for girls. Anyone would do, he wasn't fussy. It didn't matter who, and it didn't matter where ... though the back of the van proved a convenient place. In fact, Tom actually worked hard at learning to drive and passing his test so that he could take the van out and use it for his own pleasures.

It didn't take him too long to build a name for himself as a singer, either. He had a lucky break along the way.

Just after he recorded his debut single "It's Not Unusual" — which later went on to top the British Hit Parade — he was thrust into the spotlight after the American singing star P. J. Proby was pulled off a major British concert tour, for deliberately exciting his audience in a blatant sexual manner and splitting his skin-tight trousers on stage.

Tom Jones, doing almost an identical act — minus the trouser splitting — as far as the sexual excitement was concerned, replaced him ... and proved, a sensation.

"One night I was in a pub between shows having a drink," he remembered. "There was a crowd of kids outside, screaming at somebody. I figured it must have been one of the other stars on the tour. So I walked outside to take a look. The crowd nearly tore all the clothes off my back, and what clothes they did manage to grab hold of, they were ripping to shreds. Everyone wanted a piece as a souvenir.

"That was the first time I came in to contact with mass hysteria like that and I walked straight into it without knowing, it was me they were shouting for! Now it would happen all the time if I didn't take precautions."

Since those early days, Tom Jones has taken the world by storm peddling his wares of songs and sex, to become one of the world's leading superstars ... and very much in demand.

"The most important thing," he said, "is the voice. Without that there's nothing ... and I'd have no stage appeal at all. That's the only worry I ever have. It would be the worst thing that could happen to me if I ever lost my voice.

"Yet despite all that, I really am a family man. Out on stage it's different. But if I was a bachelor today, I wouldn't know who to marry, because I would find it impossible to distinguish whether the girl was in love with me, or with Tom Jones the entertainer."

The Tom Jones superstud image — albeit on stage if we are to believe him — has brought the singer his fair amount of embarrassing moments and it does have it's drawbacks if you can call them that!

"One night in Las Vegas, a girl came up on stage, opened up the front of her dress, took off her brassiere and handed it to me. I mopped my brow with it and handed it back," said Tom, ever the gentleman.

"Then another time a girl jumped up on stage and made a grab for my lower regions — and squeezed hard. Wow! One of the security guards came out on stage to pull her off, but he couldn't see what had actually happened. He was just smiling and slowly trying to pull the girl off to the wings. He was trying to help me, but I couldn't do anything — not even open my mouth.

"By the time they'd gotten her off, I was speaking to the audience about two octaves higher than usual. Boy ... she gave me a real grab!

"Anyway, not long after that incident, I was playing a theater in the round in Valley Forge, when I recognized a girl's face in the audience, though I just couldn't remember

74

who she was, or where I'd seen her before.

"Haven't I seen you before, I asked the girl, but she said nothing. She just raised her hand in the air and squeezed her fist together hard! I can still feel it!"

10
RUDOLPH VALENTINO
...Just a Gigolo?

Every pair of eyes in that crowded, sultry South American bar was fixed on the tall elegant figure of the Gaucho. He paid no attention to the faces, but stood in silence, calculating ... staring at the couple on the dance floor before him.

He was smoking now – and as he pulled hard and long on the smouldering cheroot that parted his lips, the smoke curled upwards to form a strange and haunting halo around his wide-brimmed hat. He looked menacing.

Slowly, almost deliberately, he walked across the room to the two people who had been the center of his attention – and gestured to the man to stand aside while he cut in to dance with his partner. Not a single word was exchanged, *yet* all the time the Gaucho's eyes burned penetratingly into the girl's.

Suddenly, the tightly coiled whip the Gaucho held by his side was snapped into action and he beat the other man to the floor in submission. In the next moment, he brutally seized the girl in his arms and almost forced her to dance a lazy, sensuous tango with him. When the dance was over, he pulled her even tighter to his body and kissed her violently.

... In that moment of dramatically contrived movie fire and passion, Rudolph Valentino, as the Gaucho in the film "The Four Horsemen Of The Apocalypse" became the *Greatest Lover* in the world in the eyes of millions of women. The man to whom they would have willingly surrendered ... and given their bed space – *and* a lot more besides.

It was one of the most magnificent and stunningly impactive entrances in the history of the cinema, in a film that made the twenty-six year old Italian immigrant a star. And started a legend that was to be clouded in myths and mysteries long after his premature death a mere five years later.

Valentino was different from the rest — he became the Great Lover of the silent movies at a time when women, particularly in America, were experiencing the first breeze of liberation after the First World War.

He was a fantasy figure, who oozed sex appeal from every part of his lithe body, and his larger than life presence on the screen brought dreams of desire and sleepless nights to women of all ages, and all stations in life. The image didn't discriminate.

He was a powerful symbol of virility in films, whose dramatic, almost affected, gestures sent shivers up and down every feminine back in the audience ... *and a few men's as well.* He almost raped his leading ladies with those hypnotic eyes before manhandling them into submission. He treated them brutally, but they loved him for it, and as he arrogantly dominated them, it made *their* responses even greater.

On the screen, Valentino was totally in command and it was natural to assume that in his private life, too, he was exactly the same — a womanizer and superstud. Indeed, his reputation brought women in their thousands flooding to see him, to catch a glimpse of those mesmerizing eyes, whenever he made a public appearance or attended a first night film premier.

But the image belied the man. Nothing could have been further from the truth. Although very much a ladies' man, Rudy had very little luck with women away from the film lot. There was very rarely a hint of any scandal or rumor concerning his exploits with other women. He was certainly *not* promiscuous. He was almost a tragic figure.

His first wife Jean Acker walked out on him on their wedding night, and slammed the bedroom door in his face before he even had a chance to whip off his trousers, let alone consummate the marriage. His second wife, the bi-sexual Natacha Rambova, dominated him and demanded total control over his career, so much so that she almost ruined him.

His life was dominated, too, by vicious sneers and accusations casting doubts on his own manliness, his virility and his potency. He had a preference off screen for relaxing in the company of his bachelor friends, several of whom were known homosexuals, which naturally led to innuendo and rumor that Rudy himself was aroused by members of his own sex. At one time there was even a story circulating that he was having an affair with that other "great" screen lover Ramon Novarro! Legend has it, that when Rudy died at the age of thirty-one, Novarro kept a bedroom shrine to his memory, in which were placed several dubious instruments of sexual delight and pleasure, one signed in silver by Valentino himself. Still, the rumors were the price of fame ... and Rudolph Valentino always wanted to be famous.

He was born in the small town of Castellaneta in Southern Italy on May 6th, 1895 and christened Rodolpho Alfonzo Raffaelo Pierre Filibert Gugliemi Di Valentina D'Antonguolla. His father, Giovanni, was a former cavalry officer turned vetinary surgeon; his mother, Beatrice, was the daughter of a distinguished French surgeon.

At school, he was anything but an academic, which angered his father. Indeed, the young Rodolpho spent much of his time playing truant, until his father caught him, beat him and personally escorted him back to the school room. He did, however, possess a natural talent for gymnastics, and for dancing, which was something that would help him to make a steady living later in life.

His father died when Rudy was eleven, yet because the family was comfortably off, he was allowed to continue with his education. In fact, when he left school, he was sent to the Dante Alighieri College in Taranto where he studied all aspects of agriculture. It was during this period of his higher education, that Rodolpho gained a big reputation for himself as a girl-chaser and local superstud. He was often found in very uncompromising positions with the town beauties, and on several occasions he was horsewhipped by irate fathers for dallying with their daughters' attentions.

Although he wasn't particularly clever or studious, Rudy was ambitious. He delighted in telling his friends how he would leave Italy and seek his fame and fortune abroad. He loved to talk ... and spent hours telling the same friends all about his sexual conquests, leaving little to the imagination.

At the age of eighteen, however, his ambitions got the upper hand. So he borrowed some money from an uncle and bought a one-way ticket to New York, where he was convinced he was destined to become rich. His mother was against his leaving home, yet she *did* manage to fix him up with some kind of accommodation in New York with an immigrant Italian family, before the S.S. Cleveland sailed west on December 9th, 1913 taking her son with it.

"He dreamed of owning an orange grove in California to give to his mother in Italy," said writer June Mathis, who discovered Rodolpho and gave him his first starring rôle in movies. She later became a great influence in his life. "He came to America to become a millionaire."

Two days before Christmas Day 1913, he arrived on American soil and went to live in New York's Italian ghetto — Little Italy. But he was soon disillusioned with his new life and surroundings, though the liberated young ladies fascinated him.

Rodolpho had a whole series of jobs in his early days in America. He was a refuse-collector, dishwasher and messenger boy — and ended up getting sacked from them all. Next he decided to put his agricultural training to good use, and took a job as gardener's boy on the Long Island estate of a millionaire, from which he was again dismissed within weeks of starting the job. Then, after a short spell of weeding the gardens and tending the trees in Central Park, he took any job he could lay his hands on.

Legend has it, that in order to keep warm, he stuffed old newspapers inside his tattered shirt, and that when times were really tough, he contemplated suicide.

In his spare time Rodolpho made his own entertainment and visited the cafes and bars of New York City, where he perfected his English, and observed life in general, and *the women* in particular.

However, in the spring of 1915, he discovered the charm of the city's dance-halls and cabarets, and was drawn irresistibly by their promise. It was here that the liberated American women (of all ages, of all social status and marital standing, *and* of all shapes and sizes), spent afternoons or evenings, dancing with the good-looking and immaculately dressed gigolos who lined the walls, just waiting for their services to be engaged. For a price — to be determined — a girl could choose *any* man for the duration of the session and do with him virtually what she wanted, so long as she had the money to pay. She could dance with him, sit and talk with him, or if the mood took, she could make love with him in an upstairs room or a downtown hotel.

To the young and impressionable Rodolpho, the dance-halls looked like paradise. Well, it was certainly a better way of earning a living than working in a restaurant, which was his current mode of employment. He could dance quite well, too, and with his dark, Latin good-looks, and those magnetic eyes, he was a natural. He got a job as a gigolo without any trouble and became a favorite with the women in a matter of days. He was in constant demand for his services and more and more customers asked for him by name. Within a month, Rudy was proving to be a sensation and was earning well over fifty dollars a week (no mean sum in 1915) from his job of dancing with – and on many occassions, *sleeping* with – the lonely customers. *The legend was being created!*

As his reputation increased so, too, did his ambition and it wasn't long before he quit the second rate, downtown dance-hall and moved to Maxim's, a much more sophisticated cabaret in the heart of the city. Actually at this time, Rudy wore a tight-fitting corset under his elegant evening suit, because he put on weight easily with the good life he was now able to afford and regularly enjoy.

At Maxim's he proved to be an even bigger success, and he certainly seemed to have some strange power over members of the opposite sex, who were enchanted by him. There he met Bianca de Saulles, the wife of the wealthy and highly-connected socialite, Jack de Saulles.

However, for his debut at the new cabaret, Rodolpho decided to discard his cumbersome surname. *Guglieme* was hardly a name that people would remember. Rudy needed something with flair; a name to match his reputation as a ladies' man. So he adapted his already lengthy Italian title ... and became Rodolpho di Valentina. Shortly afterwards, he teamed up with dancer Bonnie Glass and together they gave exhibitions at all the New York cabarets, and even took their stunning act out on tour. Their sensual tango was the highlight and always in great demand. With every slow and deliberate step, Rudy's reputation gained momentum.

An appearance in court, and two nights in the Tombs Prison, were soon to change all that!

He first appeared before a judge when he was called as a vital witness during the divorce proceedings Bianca de Saulles brought against her husband. Joan Sawyer, one of Rudy's former dancing partners, was named as co-respondent and he testified to their adultery.

A few weeks later, in September 1916, he was arrested on a blackmail and extortion charge and thrown into prison. He was released soon after through lack of evidence, but Rudy was convinced Jack de Saulles had "framed" him. A year later, when de Saulles was killed by his wife Bianca, Rodolpho decided to get out of town fast, before he could become involved. He left New York and joined a travelling musical show, and set off for California with the ambition of making his name in motion pictures. Things didn't quite work out to his specification, though, and he spent most of his time queuing for work as an extra at all the major studios. When he was turned down, he returned to the only trade he knew: he danced the tango in the seedy California bars and dance-halls.

However, he did manage to break into movies at long last, and made his film debut – as an extra – in the 1918 picture "Alimony".

During the following year, movie work was easier to come by and he made several films including "Eyes Of Youth", which was later to play a big part in shaping his future career. Now with regular work, Rudy was for once trying to live *down* his past

life as a "two-bit" gigolo and even refused several rôles which called for him to portray Italian dancing partners. In November, he met Jean Acker a young actress, at a Hollywood party, and within days of their meeting, they married.

Miss Acker was a strange choice of partner for Rudy. She wore her hair close-cropped like a man's and had a preference for wearing male clothes, particularly ties, which gave rise to the rumors that she was lesbian. The rumors had substance too, for she was also a protegé of the celebrated Russian actress and well-known lesbian, Nazimova — who surrounded herself with homosexuals. Natacha Rambova — Rudy's second wife — was also one of Nazimova's protegés.

His marriage to Jean Acker lasted only a few hours. Shortly before midnight on their wedding night, his wife refused his amorous advances and husbandly rights, and slammed the bedroom door in his face, rejecting him completely. The marriage was never consummated — a fact that was revealed in great detail at the divorce hearing two years later, when Rudy was at the height of his fame as the Great Lover.

Yet although his liaison with Jean Acker was a total disaster, she was at least responsible for changing his name to ... *Rudolph Valentino*.

Rudy's 1919 movie "Eyes Of Youth" led noted movie writer June Mathis to spot his great impact on the screen *and* his potential to become a great star. She had been commissioned to write the screenplay for the best-selling book "The Four Horsemen Of The Apocalypse" and was given a free-hand in choosing the stars.

"As soon as I saw Valentino", she said. "I knew there could be no other to play Julio — the Gaucho — in my screeplay. After that rôle, he was an overnight sensation."

In March 1921, when the film was released, June Mathis's words came true. The Press had a new star — and the cinema, a new sex symbol! Rudy caused so much impact on the screen, that now he could pick and choose the women he wanted to share his bed – there were certainly enough of them. Millions in fact, who formed long queues whenever and wherever the film was shown, *and* sent him 1,000 fan letters every week!

A few months later, however, he chose Natacha Rambova.

He met Natacha – whose real name was Winifred Shaughnessy – while making the film "Camille", playing opposite the legendary Nazimova. Rumors were rife that Rudy actually made passionate love to Rambova in his dressing room before being called out on set. Though whatever *did* happen in the dressing room, doubts about her hetrosexuality abounded.

Natacha was a powerful woman and throughout her relationship with Valentino – they lived together before they were finally allowed to marry – she completely dominated him, to such an extent, that she caused great friction at both MGM and Paramount studios by demanding "artistic control" over all of his movies. Rudy was totally besotted with her.

Still, in the autumn of 1921, he made the film that was to ensure his position and reputation as the world's Great Lover, forever – "The Sheik". It was a triumph ... and for the first time exploited sexual sadism and rape (albeit in the mind) on the screen. It was "romance with menace" as one writer later called it.

The women went crazy for Valentino and couldn't get enough of his penetrating eyes and sensual glares. Director Robert Florey believed that Rudy couldn't help the way he looked at women on screen, he was actually *squinting*, which was brought on by his near-sightedness. The fans would have none of it. They longed for him to carry them off to his tent in the desert and force them into sexual submission. Every one of his female fans readily associated themselves with his leading lady, Agnes Ayres. The men, far from admiring his flamboyant style, were resentful. When it came to lovemaking, Valentino outclassed them all ... and they didn't like it!

In May 1922, Valentino and Natacha were married. Eight days after the ceremony he found himself in a Los Angeles prison on a charge of bigamy. He had failed to comply with California State Law which required a divorcee to wait a full year before re-marrying. Rudy had waited for just five months.

The newspapers caught the story and it was splashed across the headlines throughout the world. The story was hot ... but it *scorched* at his trial a few weeks later when, in defense of the charge, Rudy openly admitted that he and Natacha had *not* consummated their bigamous marriage and had *not* slept together. The case was dismissed for lack of evidence of their cohabitation. The bad publicity, however, did nothing to harm his reputation with his fans. His career was intact and his new film "Blood And Sand", which almost *over*-emphasized his virility and macho-ness, was a big box-office success. Rudolph Valentino could do no wrong.

A year later, after Natacha virtually forced him to quit Paramount, he and his wife undertook an American dancing tour to raise money to pay off their mounting debts. It was sponsored by a leading cosmetic and toiletry manufacturer ... and crowds in their thousands flocked to see him on stage, demanding that he dance the infamous tango. He didn't let them down. The tour was a sensation. Vast crowds greeted his arrival at each station on the itinerary, and mobbed his car all the way to the theater! It was the same in every town the show visited, and sales of the cosmetics rocketed. To coincide with the tour, his old movies were re-released, attracting the largest audiences in history in many cities throughout the States. The Great Lover had lost none of his attraction, even though he was now not employed by a major studio. He was the *biggest star in the history of the cinema*. A veritable superstar, with the world's women falling at his feet.

Just prior to the sponsored tour, on March 14th, 1923, Rudy and Natacha had at last married, though the marriage was to last for just another two years. But for the time being, he was a slave to his wife and even insisted on wearing the chunky, platinum slave bracelet she gave him as a Christmas present. He swore his undying love – and *never* took it off. But in August 1925, she left him!

Valentino threw himself into his work and started making a new movie for United Artistes with whom he had recently signed a long contract. His co-star in "The Eagle" was the delightful Vilma Banky. With Rambova out of the way, the Press had a field day and rumors of Rudy's affair with the glamorous young star were rife, though he vehemently denied a liaison.

In November he applied for American citizenship before leaving for England to promote the new film. In London, scenes for the opening were unbelievable; women besieged the theater for hours before the star was due to arrive and tickets exchanged hands on the black market for many times their face value; *everyone* wanted to see Valentino. When at last he did show himself to the crowd, they broke through a massive police cordon and mobbed him, almost ripping the clothes from his back. He might have lost his wife ... but his fans, thousands of them, were as loyal as ever. To them – he was still The Great Lover, and always would be!

Back home in Hollywood, he struck up a friendship with the young Polish actress Pola Negri who became his mistress.

Valentino made his final movie (and some people say his *greatest*) in the summer of 1926. "Son Of The Sheik" was the sequel to his blockbusting picture "The Sheik" five years before, and the plot followed the same rules. Plenty of seduction with "menacing romance" ... and Rudy actually had his eye-lids glued back to make his eyes even more penetrating.

When the film was released in Los Angeles, he was given a standing ovation at the premiere, and he looked set for even greater adulation when he left for a promotional tour in the east, which included Chicago.

But to coincide with his personal appearance in the city, the *Chicago Tribune* took it upon itself to launch a vicious and blistering attack on his masculinity in the now legendary "Pink Powder Puff" story.

The paper's editorial writer had recently visited a local ballroom where, in the men's washroom, he found a device on the wall for dispensing pink face powder on to pink powder puffs, and men were actually using it!

The writer told the story and added "*Homo Americanus!* Why didn't someone quietly drown Rudolph Gugliemo, alias Valentino years ago?" and went on to imply that Rudy, through his image and reputation, had turned the American male into a character of effeminacy, using cosmetics – which Valentino wore on and *off* screen *and* heavy perfumes as well – and wearing slave bracelets. He concluded: "Rudy, the beautiful gardener's boy, is the prototype of the American male.

"Hell's bells. Oh sugar."

It was meant to be a tongue-in-cheek article, designed to bring a little light hearted relief for *Tribune* readers. Valentino resented every single word and challenged the writer to a boxing match just to prove his own virility and masculinity at least. When the tour reached New York, he hired the roof top of the Ambassador Hotel, and staged a boxing demonstration for the benefit of the Press.

The fight, however, never took place. A few days later on August 15th, after "The Son Of The Sheik" had opened to a tremendous reception in New York, Rudy was rushed to The Polytechnic Hospital, suffering from a ruptured appendix and a gastric ulcer. A major operation followed, during which time the hospital was besieged by thousands of eager fans waiting for news of their hero. Bulletins were even released to a waiting world via the radio! And the newspapers carried daily reports of his condition.

At 12.10 p.m. on Monday, August 23rd, 1926, Rudolph Valentino died. He was thirty-one. Just before he passed away, and now in terrible pain, he asked his doctors: "And now do I act like a pink powder puff?" The article still weighed heavily on his mind.

The world was stunned at his demise and almost immediately, rumors started to circulate. The official cause of death was peritonitis, which had set in following his operation. Few people believed it. It wasn't romantic enough for the Great Lover. So stories abounded. Some people said he had died of syphillis – perhaps it was more in keeping with the image *he* created, after all to cinema-goers he was supposed to be a stud. Another story told of his being poisoned by Bianca de Saulles, or at least, by the friends of her dead husband. Another still, said he had been shot by an outraged husband.

As the news of his death spread, one woman in London committed suicide. In New York two women attempted to kill themselves outside the hospital, and in Paris an elevator boy, at the Ritz Hotel, was found dead on his bed with a tear-stained picture of Valentino in his hands and a thousand more scattered all over the bedroom.

Rudy was laid in state at Frank E. Campbell's Broadway Funeral Parlor and New York virtually came to a stand-still as hordes of people tried to get a last glimpse at their dead hero – and pay their final respects. A crowd of well over 100,000 fought for the privilege of saying "good-bye". The city had seen nothing like it before. Pandemonium reigned. His girl friend, Pola Negri, arrived shortly afterwards and announced to the world that she and Rudy had been engaged. It was a claim made by dozens of other women, including dancer Marion Brenda.

The funeral took place on November 30th, 1926 and was almost like a state affair with thousands of people lining the streets as the procession passed by on its way to the cemetery. Rudy's body was later shipped across America where it was buried in the family crypt belonging to his old friend June Mathis. It was supposed to be only a temporary resting place – but when *she* died a year later, she was buried beside the man she had discovered and made into a great star.

The Great Lover was dead ... *but the legend lived on.*

Rudolph Valentino certainly had a power over women – why else would thousands of them flock to see his films, and mob him wherever he went? Yet, off screen, he was an enigma, and a very different personality, who was constantly haunted by accusation and rumor. He did nothing to dispel the rumors though, apart from the final

"Pink Powder Puff" incident, and many people believed that he was either bi-sexual or at least a latent, if not practising, homosexual.

He was a dream lover for millions of women, though, but never the superstud they assumed him to be.

Despite his private life, he was certainly a legend. Shortly after he died, Rudy Valee introduced a brand new song to his memory, "There's A New Star In Heaven Tonight — Rudolph Valentino". It was a smash hit.

Valentino was a bigger star ... even in death. His films were re-released over and over again, and each time, they were greeted with outstanding success at the box-office, throughout the world. Women in their hundreds flocked from all over America to pay homage to their idol's mausoleum in California. Some even chipped pieces of marble away from the shrine, to keep as souvenirs. The legend just wouldn't die! As Alice Terry, his co-star in "The Four Horsemen Of The Apocalypse" noted: "The biggest thing Valentino ever did was to die!"

11

JEAN-PAUL BELMONDO

...The Face that launched a thousand quips

Jean-Paul Belmondo hardly looks like the classic French lover epitomized by the likes of Charles Boyer and Alain Delon.

He hardly looks like a candidate for being Europe's most potent sex symbol, either, but then looks have been known to deceive. He even admits that he is not the most attractive man in the world and often refers to himself as being downright "ugly". Still, there's no denying it — he certainly possesses something which has a very strange effect on women.

His dresser once told a magazine that "nobody could call him beautiful, but he is the embodiment of the anti-homosexual."

Jean-Paul Belmondo would never win a place in any good looks guide. His legs are distinctly bandy and far too short for his six foot frame, and his face — which he calls "the ugly mug of a boxer" — is best referred to as "well lived in". One newspaper described it perfectly: "Close set eyes, large squashed nose, lips like bicycle tyres, a spade shaped jaw." Yet the same paper had no hesitation in naming Belmondo as one of the Top Ten sex symbols in the entire world, and acclaimed him a veritable superstud.

Jean-Paul's face has actually helped to make his fortune, and a fair sized reputation with the ladies. However, when he was studying at the Paris Conservatoire, his professor Pierre Dux took him to one side and told him a few facts of life. "Resign yourself, mon petit: with that face you are doomed. Nobody will ever believe *you* could get the girl."

Belmondo had other ideas, and spent the next twenty-odd years — on and particularly off the screen — proving Dux was wrong.

"For years afterwards, everytime I did an interview, I said that Pierre Dux said I'd never play romantic rôles,'' said Jean-Paul. ''Eventually, I ran across him in Paris. 'For Christ's sake,' he said. 'Stop telling the papers I said you'd never make it with girls. You make me look like a real idiot.'

''To a certain degree, though, I suppose Pierre was right. Women would not have fluttered an eyelid at an ugly man like me thirty years ago. But they have changed their outlook to men, they now like us rough and tough.''

There have certainly never been any doubts about Belmondo's toughness. In almost every movie he's made, he has insisted on undertaking his own stunt work.

''Well, I like doing stunts,'' he says, ''and if I hadn't been an actor I'd like to have been a stunt man. The only trouble is, I have to pay my own insurance since producers won't cover me. But I never do anything really dangerous.''

The word ''dangerous'' to Belmondo, covers a multitude of sins. Several years ago, he actually rode a motorcycle across a high wire that was slung between the rafters at the top of a circus tent ... *without a net!* It was for a charity benefit night at the famous Cirque d'Hiver, and half-way across the tightrope, the bike's engine stalled! Jean-Paul also brushed aside the fact that the day before the event took place, his instructor, attempting the same feat, had fallen and broken his back!

Over the years, the rough and tough image Belmondo projects has certainly paid dividends when it comes to women. His track record has attracted world headlines and his amorous adventures have taken in such desirable actresses as Brigitte Bardot, Jean Seberg, Claudia Cardinale, Dany Robin, Joanna Shimkus and Filipino beauty Minda Feliciano ... to name but a handful. In 1975, he was even rumored to be having an affair with Greek millionairess Christina Onassis after they had been seen out together in Paris, on several occasions.

But his most famous romance was with Swiss actress Ursula Andress, who became his live-in lover for seven publicity-filled years. Indeed, throughout France the affair was referred to as ''La Grande Amour'', by the romantics, or ''L'affaire Scandaleuse'' by the narrow-minded.

Their liaison first hit the headlines in 1965 when she left her husband John Derek after nine years of marriage. Belmondo was cited in their divorce case as co-respondent after he had left his wife and three children to set up a love-nest with the actress in Paris. Three years later, their affair was openly criticized by a French High Court judge when Ursula was named as the other woman in Jean-Paul's own divorce hearing. In his summing up, the judge spoke of Belmondo's ''intimate and guilty relations'' with Miss Andress, and added: ''Their public behavior was notorious.''

She reacted strongly: ''Morals? To me it is much more moral to live with the man you love *without* a piece of paper than to live legally in an atmosphere of boredom which can turn to hate.''

She told one newspaper about the secret of the affair's success. ''We never get bored no matter how much we are in each other's company. I don't mean we've invented more love-making positions than most people or anything like that. It's purely that we've found so many things in life that are interesting to share.

''Perhaps one of the reasons why our love survives, is because of that freedom to part when we please. But I put it down to our trust in each other.

''If Jean-Paul did sleep with another girl, though, that would be the end.''

Their romance lasted until April 1975 during which time Ursula boasted that neither she nor Jean-Paul had ever been unfaithful to each other. "How many legally married couples can claim that," she added. Obviously the French judge's words had left a bitter scar. But she later admitted that they were so much in love that she had willingly become Jean-Paul's slave and maybe that drove them apart. "Suddenly we both realized our love for each other was so passionate it was stifling", she said. "I didn't have any personality any more and I was at his beck and call the whole time. But we were lovers for seven years, and it was idyllic."

Jean-Paul Belmondo has been one of his country's top actors now since he first burst on to the movie screen in 1959 with a major starring rôle in the picture "Bout Des Souffle" ("Breathless"). He was hailed as France's answer to James Dean, called the "new Bogart" and became an overnight success with an appeal and charm all of his own.

"New blood, new looks, new vitality, new fluidum, new eroticism," was how Marlene Dietrich described him, which just about said it all. Who needed good looks anyway? Belmondo had his own kind of sex-appeal. Raw and unsophisticated – which made women go weak at the knees just looking at his leather-bound face. Men, however, could see nothing in his attraction.

"The trouble with men," said Ursula Andress in happier climes, "is that they can't understand another man's attraction. They keep getting good-looks mixed up with sex-appeal – and they have got nothing to do with each other. Jean-Paul's fantastic." It was a sentiment echoed by hundreds of women all over Europe.

Brigitte Bardot called him "amazing". Sophia Loren added that he had a "magnetic attraction", and even actor Omar Sharif, himself a front-runner in the playboy stakes and his co-star on "The Burglars", admitted that Jean-Paul had something extraordinary about him, and added in way of explanation that he was "charming and easy-going".

Actress Anna Karina – they made "Une Femme Est Une Femme" together – told a newspaper: "He's not pretty, but he's vulgar!" She didn't elaborate on his vulgarity, however.

Jean-Paul Belmondo was born in Neuilly-sur-Seine, Paris in 1933. His father Paul Belmondo was Italian, and a celebrated monument sculptor. He was a distinguished member of the Academie des Beaux Arts *and* the Legion of Honour. His French mother was infinitely tolerant of her rebellious young son, and humorous, with a passion for the circus. "She always used to take me," recalled Jean-Paul.

Belmondo was a rebel in his young days. At school, his only achievements were on the field of sport – he was a good boxer and excelled at soccer, too. He attended Paris's famous Ecole Alsatienne ... and was duly expelled.

At the age of sixteen, he developed a minor lung infection, and was sent to the central region of Auvergne, where he took a great interest in bicycle racing ... and girls.

"What were my parents going to do with me?" he once asked an American magazine. "They knew there wasn't any point in sending me back to school. I wanted to be a professional bicycle racer or a boxer or a soccer player, or something. But they put their foot down at that!

"I never had a complete formal education. I left home at sixteen even though my parents wanted me to continue with my schooling. My father had a manufacturer friend who promised to give me a wonderful job – but I had to start at the bottom, wrapping packages and I couldn't even wrap packages.

"When I told my father I wanted to be an actor, he was very much against the idea and tried to dissuade me. When he realized I was determined, he sent me to see another friend of his, André Brunot at the Comedie Francaise and I had a private little audition backstage in his dressing room. Afterwards, *he* called my father and said never in his life had he seen anyone with so little talent and begged him to persuade me to give up plans for the theater.

"Then at the Conservatoire, they told me right away I'd never be anything but a *valet de comedie*. Well I didn't mind so much, I never expected to be a star, just to act, and make a living in the theater. But what I didn't see was why I couldn't get the girl once in a while. When my professor said: 'Just look at your kisser', I asked him to come cruising around with me some night and he could see for himself whether girls liked me or not." They *adored* him, and Jean-Paul was rarely seen without a girl on his arm. Things haven't changed. He actually had his first sexual experience at the age of fifteen. He told an English newspaper all about it.

"It was in the cellar of the apartment block where I lived with my parents. The girl lived not far from me. We were about the same age and she was madly in love with me.

"I persuaded her to come down to my cellar and, after making several promises which I had no intention of keeping, she even agreed to lie down on the mattress.

"After I had sworn eternal love to her and given her one or two little kisses as an hors d'oeuvre, I got closer ... so much closer.

"We were both trembling but I had the advantage because she was not to know

89

that I was as new to this as she was.

"She didn't talk and neither did I. It was such a wonderful new experience that I didn't dare move for fear of breaking the spell.

"And so it was that she suddenly realized *where* I was. She was overcome with panic and began to scream and hit me.

"At last she stopped and ran up the staircase.

"The next morning, I saw the little victim glowing with happiness coming towards me. We went back to the cellar where we started all over again, but this time, there was no screaming ... and she didn't run away."

Girls have been running *towards* him and coming back for more ever since.

In 1952, Jean-Paul Belmondo married a dancer whom he re-christened Elodie because he didn't like her original name. Their marriage lasted fifteen years until he discovered the delights of Ursula Andress after they worked together on the film "Les Tribulations D'Un Chinois En Chine".

He actually started his acting career, after graduating from the Conservatoire, in 1956 by touring the French provinces in various plays and productions, sometimes playing to a mere handful of people in a local church hall which doubled as a theater.

Back in Paris, he landed several theater rôles and started appearing in low-budget movies. His film debut came in 1957 in "A Pied A Cheval Et En Voiture", followed by "Sois Belles Et Tais-toi". In 1958, he made his name on the French stage in the play "Oscar", which led to his playing the part of a gangster in "Bout Des Souffle" – the film that made him a star. In a few years, Jean-Paul Belmondo had emerged as the most popular actor in France and one of the country's highest paid as well! And with good reason. Film critic Pauline Kael, reviewing one of his movies said in 1963 that Belmondo "is probably the most exciting new presence on the screen since Brando; nobody holds the screen this way without enormous reserves of talent ..." *and* she might well have added, *enormous reserves of sex appeal*, for besides becoming Europe's most dynamic new actor, Jean-Paul Belmondo was also making his reputation as one of Europe's most devastating sex-symbols and lady-killers. Rumors about his off-screen liaisons with *all* of his leading ladies swept around the world.

"Outside Ursula," he reacted to them, "I have never been attracted to my partners I act with. Every time I make a film, the magazines always say I am having an affair with my co-star. Actresses, are as they should be – effective on screen, but too much trouble to bother with off screen. They are more often than not far too concerned with their appearance and careers."

Still, the man with a rockery for a face was not only getting good reviews ... he was also getting the girls!

Since then, Jean-Paul Belmondo has been called "The Sexiest Man On The Screen" by one newspaper and "Europe's Number One Sex Symbol" by another. He has managed to land the girl in over sixty major movies all of which have been massive box-office successes throughout Europe, where, quite simply, he reigns supreme. Such is his appeal, however, that movie makers from Hollywood have tried to lure him to America, but he has turned them all down. He speaks very little English and has no intention of learning. Whenever he makes a film for an English-speaking audience, he learns his lines phonetically and speaks them parrot-fashion. "I suppose I could learn, but what for? English-speaking audiences may be bigger than French ones, but I'm quite happy. Anyway, I don't want to be typed as a foreigner, that doesn't interest me."

Jean-Paul's secret of success on the screen is fairly easy to define. "In the early days when I was trying to become well-known, I considered I had an ugly mug," he told a French film magazine. "Well ... it seems I was wrong. My mug came in at the right moment. They needed it. In 1960, the days of Valentino, Tyrone Power and Cary Grant were already finished. I arrived on the scene with my broken nose, my relaxed style, wearing a leather jacket. I spoke in a natural way, not like someone in a book and I think people were waiting for me. It fitted in with the changeover from one epoch to another, the end of the dreamy-eyed bourgeoisie. Bardot, who also played in a relaxed manner, was another symptom of the times."

... And like Belmondo, Brigitte Bardot, too, went on to become a sex symbol throughout the world.

Yet his success in conquering some of the world's most delectable women is harder to define. Several journalists have actually attributed it to the fact that *they* believe him to be a woman-hater. It is something they say, he radiates from the big screen. Belmondo laughs at the idea.

"Well, that's really a tall-story. It must come from a lady of the Women's Lib movement who is short of victims.

"Believe me, even in love scenes on film, I appreciate girls who do their jobs properly, who are sufficiently professional in front of the camera to remain sincere, for as long as it takes. I'm not very keen on those who flutter their eye lashes, call for the powderpuff and wonder whether they're being photographed at the right angle. But as for passion in bed ... it's not my style, nor is turning my lovelorn, empty gaze on a girl. No-one would believe in it."

Quite simply he adores women and admits to having his very own approach to love. He told an English magazine – "There's an art to lovemaking. Love is a build up. There are several stages. First and foremost ... passion. Then you must get to know the other person. You begin to understand her, and only later do you decide to live together.

"Love is like a volcano. It begins with a great passion but it can lie dormant ready to erupt at any moment. In any true love affair, there's always passion.

"I like a woman to have her own personality. An ideal woman for me is intelligent, beautiful, sweet but not boring. I couldn't stand a woman who accepts *everything*. I like a fighter who can spark a man's life.

Although he has no intention of getting married again, Jean-Paul has every intention of sampling as many women as he possibly can ... and he has even developed his very own technique of seduction. He told a Sunday newspaper about it.

"You go into a dark club, find a girl and gently push her skirt down to her knees. Then you say – heavens, you've got smashing legs. But don't let everyone see.

"Then leave your hand on her knee as if you forgot it, until she gets annoyed. Next look into her eyes and say: 'Excuse me. I am unpardonable, but I am happy you are so chaste and cautious. Not many girls are these days. It's a dirty dog trick, but it works. Ninety-nine per cent of women feel forced to point out that they are NOT so chaste!"

Who could blame them, either, faced with one of Europe's most potent sex symbols?